Even the Dead Rise Up

Francis McKee

Even the Dead Rise Up

Book Works

Escribir es un contrato con la muerte

(John Torres, *Undead*, 2013)

Contents

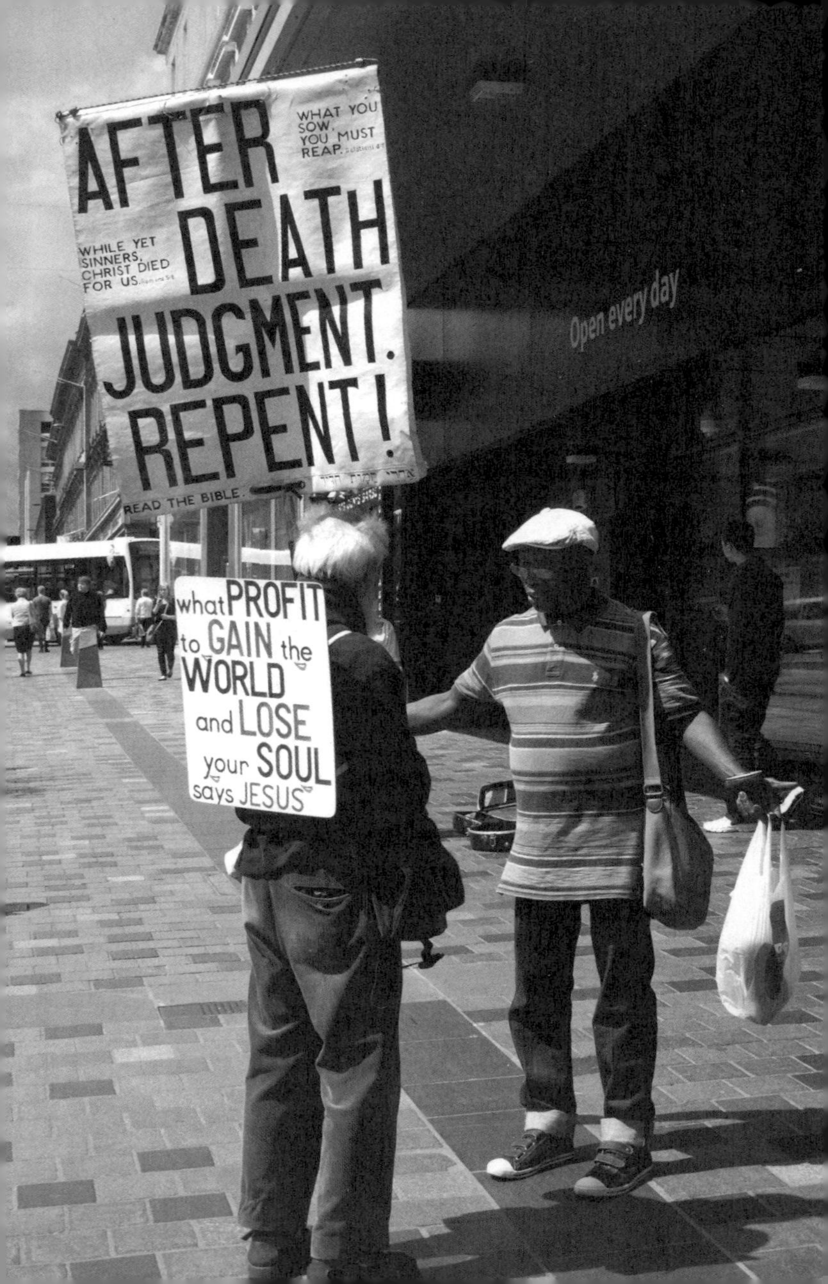
AFTER DEATH JUDGMENT. REPENT!
WHAT YOU SOW, YOU MUST REAP.
WHILE YET SINNERS, CHRIST DIED FOR US.
READ THE BIBLE.
Open every day
what PROFIT to GAIN the WORLD and LOSE your SOUL says JESUS

Author's Note

The sun is rising in Glasgow now: 6.07am and I can hear the first stirrings of the Crowne Plaza Hotel. Out here on the perimeter of Europe, perched above the Clyde, this is the end of one world and the threshold of another. The city below is dull red under the morning light and, looking at it, I sense the dread in my belly, the need finally to get this all in print, still wary of everything since I returned from Paris.

Of course I'm late with the text but that doesn't matter any more. The thing is. I am born again. Nothing compares to that. Not what I was. Dead, but somehow here again with new eyes, wide awake.

Gavin booked me in here last night and he'll be on the train by now. He spent most of the week trying to get me to finish up. Even brought in enough shopping for a month, and a Tascam d40 so that I could just dictate text, which he then emailed to London where it was transcribed and laid out. Like some wayward addict I kept finding ways to fill the time with other things: my day job, references for ex-students, feeding the cats, answering urgent emails... So now I have two days and three nights to complete the book. He said it was worth it and the hotel had a weekend deal so it would get me out of the house and away from my usual bad habits. I had to finish by Monday or they would move on: tired of waiting, press release already out, a deadline set for the launch of the remaining books in the series. They could use the money better elsewhere too...

Beyond all of that is the grief. She is no longer there and never will be. Not much else matters. Behind me in the room the computer is playing 'Gaeta's Lament' on repeat:

Alone she sleeps in the shirt of man
With my three wishes clutched in her hand
The first that she be spared the pain
That comes from a dark and laughing rain
When she finds love may it always stay true
This I beg for the second wish I made too
But wish no more
My life you can take
To have her please just one day wake
To have her please just one day wake

'The Stump Serenade'. It's still the only song

I can bear to hear. It draws me back to those mournful months when I realised I was slowly disappearing, my whole life evaporating... Up here on the twenty-first floor, looking out onto the streets beyond the motorway, I'm struggling to spot people anywhere.

This started with an eye test. I'd fallen over in the middle of a conversation and then got up and kept talking. Everyone ignored it and we put it down to tiredness. But my eyes were also not true. There were black outs and blind spots, streaming tears and unidentified artefacts. So I had an eye test. A young optician filled a computer screen with images of my retina – vast orange planets floating like gas giants in a distant nebula. He tried to tell me the right eye was poor and deteriorating. Still, he was trying to say, it would last my remaining lifetime. It couldn't be said. He was afraid to put that into words. Not something to drop easily on a customer. I didn't mind: it was good to know that the right eye was sticking by me.

The problem was that he could find nothing wrong with my eyes, apart from natural wear and tear. There were no good reasons for the black outs and blind spots. A year later that hasn't changed. If anything they're worse since I was pepper sprayed. It's difficult, though, to explain how those physical symptoms tipped me into another world.

Everyone, of course, likes to think of my recent interests as research – something to discuss within the context of 'hauntology' or a potential exhibition. It's less embarrassing for them. But the art world is just a mouth full of rotten teeth now and I don't care about making a career move. This has gone much further than research or good material for a presentation. They know nothing of this.

I glance across the room and Anna is sitting by the other window, looking east – what does she see? The skin on her bare arms shimmers in the light, teeming with weird energies.

I start to make my way across the crowded room. *there's this man...* Plenty of elbows and shoving. *move!* Boots on the bed. *this is what we want. fuck you too.* A dig in the ribs and a kidney punch. *mind yourself.* Anna's gone when I get there. *packaged horse.*

I'm on the floor looking at the leg of the bed. It's very clean underneath. Sunlight is playing on the carpet fibres and a radio is on, from the computer I suppose, a voice describing something. 'I looked around the house and saw things. I saw the tile on my floor. I saw two chopsticks crossed. I saw ferns outside. I saw a serrated knife. Things of that sort.' This is the best part of a blackout, peaceful and childlike. 'And I drew them on music paper with sine waves, in other words the waves would go up and down, drawing in the air these objects. And the hammock was simply one of the objects I drew...'

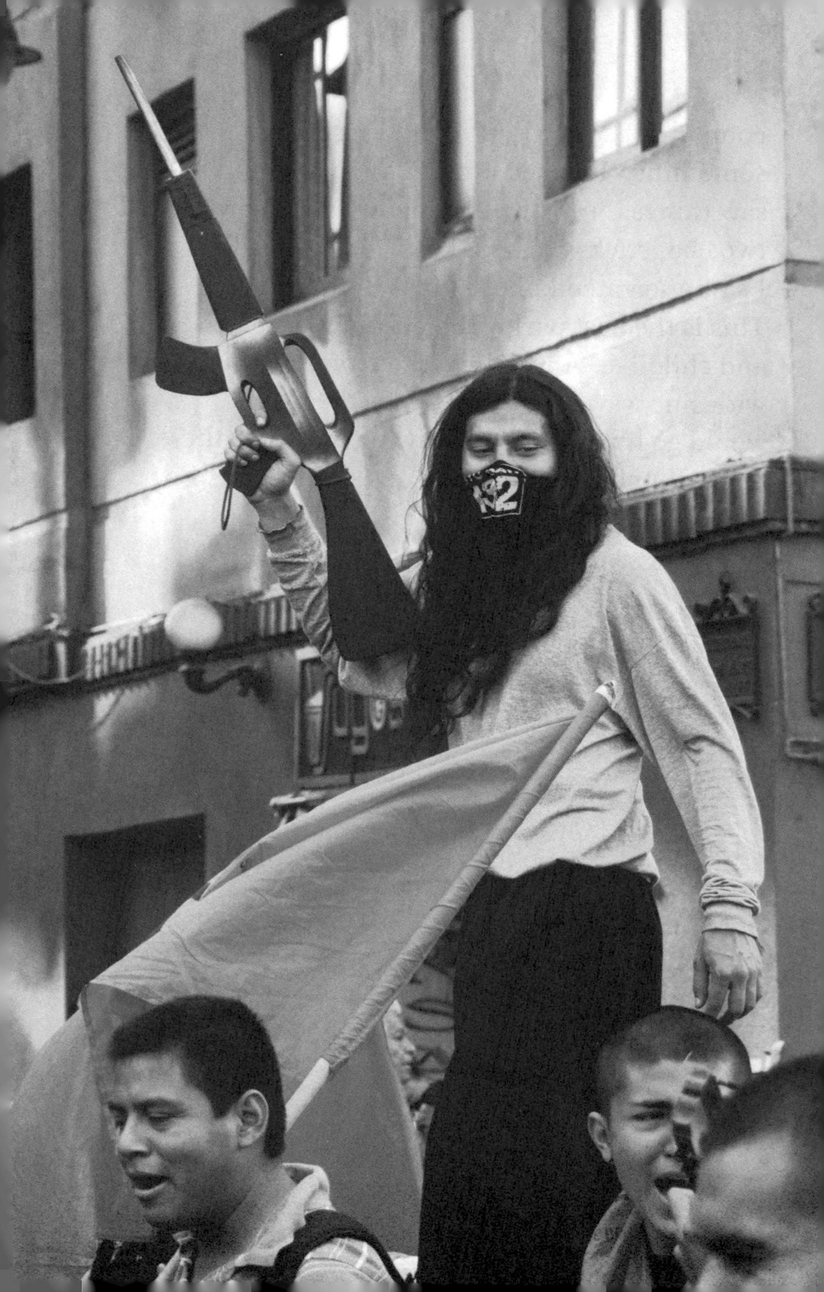

January

I step off the pavement into the road. Weaving past policemen and the protest organisers that are spread across the street I walk directly into the path of the oncoming marchers. They come straight towards me, their arms linked, banners and placards massed above them. Someone near the centre of the line wields a megaphone and the protestors around him already have their jawlines set, ready for the photographers.

I watch them approach, the camera to my eye. A 35mm prime lens is wide enough to capture the line, but tight enough to generate energy in the picture. The lens makes it appear they are further away when, in fact, they are almost on top of me. I begin to walk backwards, matching their pace, being careful not to trip or reverse into the police.

The protesters seem to have emerged from thin air. It's Sunday in Mexico City and the main streets are closed to cars so that bicycles can enjoy the centre. I was watching the cyclists from a balcony listening to the radio as families drifted by, waving to pedestrians. The drifters would be occasionally overtaken by groups of serious bikers who flashed past, neon sticks glowing on their spokes even in the noon sunlight. A news bulletin excitedly interrupted the music to declare that the '14 liberados' had successfully infiltrated the final groups of cyclists and would soon be approaching Alameda park at the rear of the event.

I was there by the time they turned the corner at Reforma and began to head towards the Zócalo. Now as I focus on the line, it suddenly dissolves and a smaller band of protestors march forward – the liberados themselves. They look directly at the lens and raise their fists in an almost weary mixture of victory and defiance. One of them, in a flat cap and black T-shirt, looking like a small Bryan Robertson from AC/DC, quite daintily holds a hand-written placard across his midriff. The placard reads 'Ser llamado amenaza x un tirano es motivo de orgullo' – 'to be called a threat by a tyrant is a source of pride'.

Three of the marchers have taped their mouths closed – perhaps a reference to articulo 362, a ruling that strips them of the normal rights of a citizen even after their release. The liberados are the last protesters to be released after a series of arrests in December, when a demonstration against the new president Enrique Peña Nieto descended into chaos. Charges of vandalism and inciting a disturbance didn't hold up in the courts and the whole judicial procedure was riddled with flaws. The protesters argued that the arrests were arbitrary and without substance.

Looking at the marchers walking towards me that argument makes sense. The liberados are a strangely mixed bunch. One man, in a slouch hat, looks much older than the others; another all white in jeans, T-shirt and baseball cap sports a white and blue tartan jacket and a cream-ish coloured fanny pack; a third barely in his twenties in cut-offs is pushing a bike (camouflage?): they seem to have nothing in common apart from their initial desire to demonstrate and their arrest.

The number of marchers behind them swells. This has been well planned. Suddenly a slender young guy, faced wrapped in a scarf, is raised aloft in the centre of the marchers and he's brandishing an automatic rifle. There's an enormous cheer and a ripple of fear spreads through the street. The gun is a cardboard cut-out, but that seems unimportant. It's a signal of where things will go under this new government.

*

Eventually the marchers disperse and filter back through the streets in couples or small groups. It's hard to dilute the adrenalin at first. Every sense is heightened: everything is significant. Then you crash and exhaustion floods the system. I slow down, languid now, stopping every few metres to investigate the street stalls.

The sheer industry of the bootleggers in Mexico City has always been a source of joy for me. At one point every street was lined with stalls selling CDs or DVDs. The attention to detail was remarkable: in Tepito there were stalls that sold only discs while neighbouring stalls sold insert cards and jewel cases for any film or album you could imagine. The stalls that dominated the Centro Histórico were where I started to learn Spanish. The sellers there had time on their hands and they were willing to talk. Their stalls often went beyond the quest to gather the most recent releases and sell them cheap. There were specialist stalls that demonstrated a level of passion and knowledge that you could not find any more in retail stores. One stall – I suspect it was famous in a quiet way across the city – was in Calle Francisco, close to Eje Central and Calle Dolores, the city's single-block Chinatown. Two young guys ran it, selling only art movies, listing the films under a filing system based on directors. There you could find every film by Jean-Luc Godard, or Fellini, Eisenstein, David Lynch, Hitchcock – it was a street library, an everyman's archive of film history. '¿Cuánto cuesta? Veinte, o tres por cinquenta…' these were the words that led me into Spanish. On another corner near El Globo, with its utopia of doughnuts and churros, a seller traded only in Cuban music – Sexteto Habanero, Benny Moré, Arsenio Rodríguez and the miniature descargas of Cachao. In one conversation it was possible to undertake a crash course in pre-revolutionary Cuba and, on a slow day, to extract an additional lecture on the impact of Pérez Prado in Mexico.

Now I'm looking for *House*, a box set, but the season isn't complete yet and they urge me to try *Battlestar Galactica*. 'You will love it. It's not *Star Wars* or *Trek*. It's much darker, much more adult, *más intelligente*. It has the cruelty and the rage of George Bush after twin towers but set in another galaxy. The dialogue is amazing...'

They're right. It's about humans that inhabit a group of planets known as the Twelve Colonies and worship the Lords of Kobol, gods almost identical to our own ancient Greek pantheon.

Once the colonies were engaged in a war with the Cylons, a cybernetic race originally invented by humans. The Cylons were defeated and their survivors were quarantined on distant planets. Now they have returned, after decades of development, and are led by superior machines that look just like real people. They destroy all the human battleships except one: the creaky old Battlestar Galactica, commanded by Admiral Adama. Now it's his task to save the human race and he rallies the crew by declaring they will light out for a mythical planet known as 'Earth'.

The makers of *Battlestar* determined that both humans and machines would reach Earth together after a truce and found a race that would effectively be our fabled ancestors. The classical references are already embedded in their names: Captain Lee 'Apollo' Adama who loves Kara 'Starbuck' Thrace; the lesser characters – Felix Gaeta, Karl Agathon, Galen Tyrol, and Anastasia; and in their cultural keystones – the Book of Pythia, and the tomb of Athena near the Gates of Hera.

So the plot is thick with Greek myth, a storyline arc lifted from Virgil's *Aeneid*, flavoured with Massachusetts laden sea shanties ('I always dream to drown at sea') and displaced characters from *Moby Dick*. Religions in the story draw on everything from Mormon beliefs to Hebraic, Christian and Hindu theologies, spliced together with esoteric references to *The Cloud of Unknowing* and the Grail legends of Roslyn Chapel. It's a heady cocktail, overloaded and listing badly, like the *Galactica* herself in the final days of her voyage.

So I go back and buy the rest of the series. By the time I get to Glasgow Starbuck and Apollo have reached Earth, though Starbuck, of course, died long before. It was, as you may know, her avatar that guided everyone to this planet.

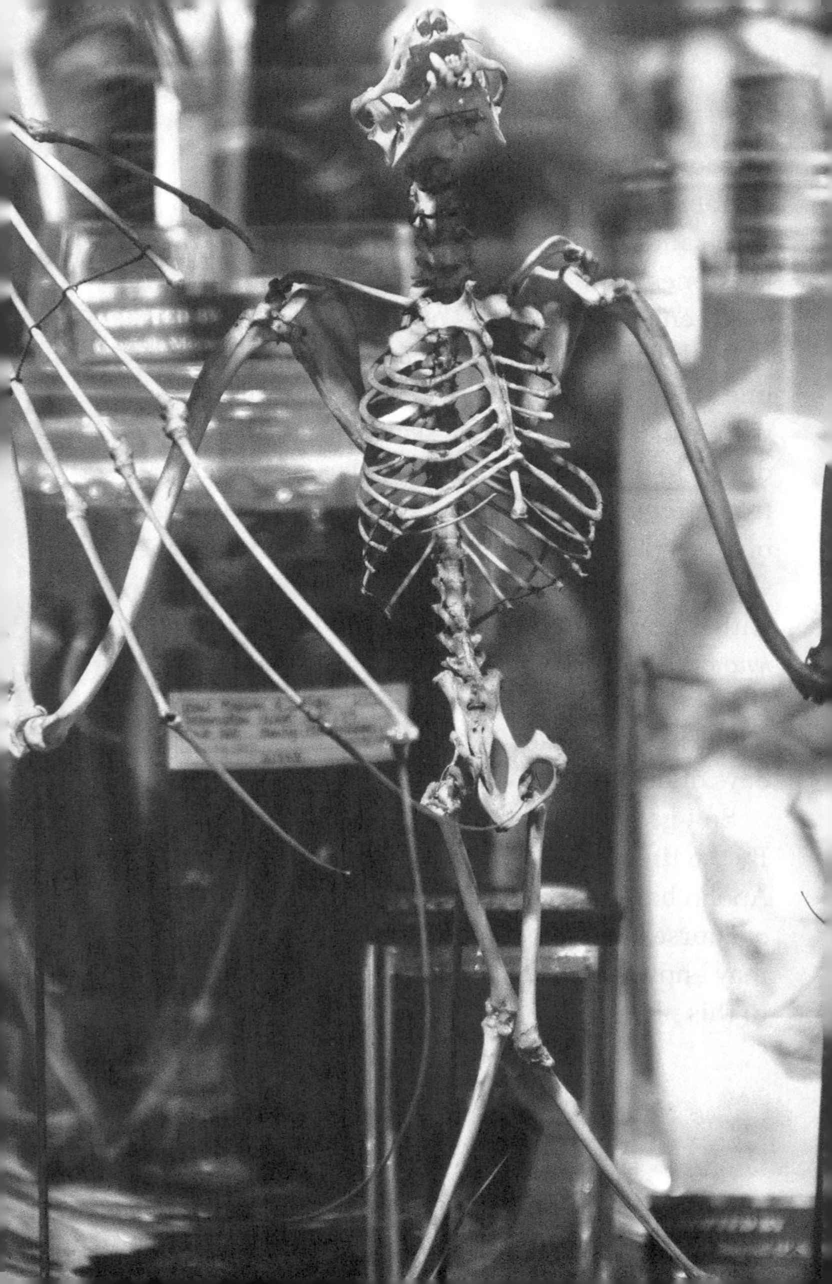

The church was actually a converted townhouse that looked bare and austere in the cold twilight. Twin pillars around the door gave a sense of grandeur, but the door itself had a light metal frame that opened on a buzzer system. Inside, the walls were hung with old photographs of spirit apparitions, double exposures and some of the finer discharges of ectoplasm.

A man sat in the corridor by a small table collecting the entrance fee. I dropped the three pounds on a plate with green felt lining and he pointed down the stairs towards the basement. 'There's tea and a biscuit – get some now because the hatch closes when it starts.'

Downstairs there was a canteen like any other built in the 1970s or 1980s, a serving hatch at one end, a long rectangular room filled with tables and plastic chairs and toilets at the other end. The only concession to the spirit world was a medium-sized black and white portrait of an American Indian in full headdress.

People were scattered around various tables in groups of two or three, the odd loner like myself too. When I queued for tea though there was some friendly banter and the man behind the counter insisted I take a biscuit pointing out that I'd paid for it.

The kitchen shutter came down quickly after that and everyone was invited to form a circle of chairs in the centre of the space. We did that and, looking around, we resembled nothing more than a typical cross-section of bus passengers, forced to disembark unexpectedly, our coats on the chairs behind us.

The medium was flanked by two staff from the church but she stood out from us all, dressed in a loose black top and skirt with a dark necklace – muted but just enough to hint at the great tradition of the séance. While we settled, one of the church organisers introduced her, explaining that they invited a different medium each week and were honoured this week to have someone they had admired for a long time. She would also take a service on Sunday and would be available for individual readings on the following Monday and Tuesday. But before we started the law required that he read the statement printed on the laminated sheet in his right hand:

You have paid to witness a Demonstration of Mediumship. This demonstration is a form of experiment; no claims are made and results cannot be guaranteed. You are not guaranteed a personal message. You may see or hear things which you may not have experienced before. If any of you feel you may be vulnerable you should leave now and your entrance fee will be refunded.

We looked at each other quickly as if checking for a dramatic reaction but no one budged. We settled further into our chairs and turned our attention to the medium who had begun to radiate authority. She let the silence build and then started to talk to us.

We all went to school as children and they told us we were being educated. But that wasn't true. There was a world of spirit around us at every moment and they never mentioned it: a world that touches on our everyday lives that they denied to us. And so, everything you've ever been taught is wrong.

We have to go back to the beginning and acknowledge that world of spirit. And this meeting this evening, this circle, is all about developing what is already within you, developing the ability to recognise spirit around you and the ability to interact with it.

*

We're divided into pairs and we have to sense messages for each other. I fail miserably. The woman I'm partnered with is from a Scottish protestant background and the names that come to her are Ian, Andy, William, but my life has been filled with Seamuses, Patricks and Seans. My first lesson: it's polite to take a message and rude to reject it. You never know if it has a wider significance.

The medium comes around to each group and listens carefully. She asks me if it's my first time and when I nod she explains that I will find it very difficult: I'm a man, a very rational and reserved man. So I'm closed to the spirits, locked down and defensive. She has a point. But, like Scully and the Fox, I want to believe.

*

Even as I write this I realise that Fox Mulder probably contained a reference to the Fox sisters – Margaret and Kate Fox – who established many of the founding principles of spiritualism when they became known across the United States in 1848 for 'rapping' and communicating with spirits.

As word spread of their abilities they were sent to Rochester to stay with their older sister Leah and their brother David. Two radical Quakers, Amy and Isaac Post, quickly alerted the rest of the Rochester Quaker community to the girls' powers. It was this convergence of an emerging mediumistic phenomenon and a radicalised religious community that linked the spiritualist movement to issues such as the abolition of slavery, temperance and equality for women.

While the Fox sisters went on to fame and then notoriety, other mediums began to seize the public's attention. One of the most important was Achsa Sprague, born in Plymouth Notch, Vermont, in 1827 and bed-bound with rheumatic fever by the time she was twenty. It took six years for her to recover and gain mobility, a fact she attributed to spiritual intercession. In 1854 she began to tour the United States, partaking in public sessions where she would fall into a trance while various spirits spoke through her. This might all sound a little dry, but she cut a spectacular figure in these appearances. It was unheard of for a respectable young woman to travel alone across America at the time. Sprague not only travelled widely but pitched up in towns and cities where lodging was offered by star-struck admirers before she addressed large crowds of people. Witnesses say she dressed in bright, richly coloured clothes and, in the best-known photograph of her, she wears a multi-striped dress that radiates energy even in the monotone image. In *Radical Spirits*, Ann Braude cites a letter from one of Achsa's admirers, advising the young woman that 'Were I a medium lecturer, female, I would dress so as not to attract attention with outlandishness in hat, frock, wristbands, and country girl flamishness.' He goes on to comment on her 'innumerable flashy ribbons' and a hat with 'Northern light streaks'.

Sprague must have had the impact of a Hendrix or Prince, arousing her audience as she channelled messages from another world. And these messages were not trivial as those of the Fox sisters had become when fame brought them into rich households where amused

gence of spiritualist activists in the nineteenth century. At first I'm surprised how concise it is and that it references Ann Braude's *Radical Spirits.*

> *Braude says: 'Spiritualists believed individuals could serve as vehicles of truth because each embodied the laws of nature in his or her being. Such individualism laid the foundation for Spiritualism's rejection of male headship over women – or indeed of any individual over any other – whether in religion, politics or society... The movement viewed the individual as the ultimate vehicle of truth.'*

(three times someone drove by at night & shot out our windows.)

Then J.L.'s argument takes a twist at the end.

> *Well, Spiritualism may have helped some women find 'a voice'. But it is doubtful that it was their voice. No way. The voices found were, probably, either the voice of the Devil or his demon helpers. And these demonic spirits are still moving the lips of many in the so-called 'womens' rights'/feminist/'pro-choice' movement. – J.L.*

(Gasoline was poured under our back door & ignited three times. Twice while the clinic was occupied, causing patients to be evacuated.)

This essay first turned up on a website called *The American View*, but this time it's pasted into a blog run by 'Timothy', who sets out his stall right away:

> *TRUTHSEEKER24'S ANTI-N.W.O. CORNER*
> *Pro-God, Pro-Life, anti-New World Order, Anti-Secret Societies, Pro-Civil Liberties, anti-Torture, anti-National ID Card, Pro-Family, pro-Constitution, Pro-Republic, Anti-Neo Conservativism, Pro-Net Neutrality, Pro-Home Schooling, Anti-Voting Fraud, Pro-Good Israelis & Pro-Good Palestinians, Anti-Human Trafficking, Pro-Health Freedom, Anti-Codex Alimentarius, Pro-Action, Anti-Jesuit Order, Pro-9/11 Truth Movement, Anti-Genocide, and Pro-Gun. My name is Timothy and I'm from the state of Virginia.*

(two home-made bombs were left on our doorstep after hours, causing damage & closing the clinic.)

J.L. was likely to have been John Lofton (1941–2014), a 'recovering Republican who never went to college' as one memorial tribute put it:

John D. Lofton, Jr.... was among other things, the most unabashed Christian I have ever met. He was the type that insisted on taking every thought captive to Christ, even if your thought would not go willingly. John will be remembered by many as an 'American paleoconservative' political commentator and editor of Michael Peroutka's The American View *radio program.*

The author of that tribute points out that Lofton's political and religious position in later life was determined by a historical perception that American values lay with the pioneers of the Mayflower and that the constitution (and Abraham Lincoln's role) corrupted those original principles:

All too many books that have fundamentally altered the course of my thinking were recommended reads by John Lofton. The very first of this sort was a book entitled The Basic Symbols of American Political Tradition. *The nub of the book: 'America' was not founded by the Constitution, rather Christianity was planted on this soil in 1620 with the Mayflower Compact. Since then, there have been enemies at work to uproot it.*

The first time I read the article it was a garbled cut and paste version in a forum. The introductory paragraphs were missing and it was only later, when I searched for it again, that I found the complete essay and realised it was written to mark the death of Betty Friedan:

BETTY FRIEDAN pushed for, we are told, among other things, 'sex-neutral help-wanted ads'. Feminism icon Betty Friedan, an early advocate of murdering innocent unborn babies – she founded the National Association For The Repeal Of Abortion Laws in 1968 – has died. Eleanor Smeal, a fellow-feminist, says of Friedan that she left 'a legacy that's living beyond her wildest dreams in the 1960s'.

Well, yes, she did leave a legacy but it was more of a nightmare than a mere dream. The 'womens' rights'/feminist/'pro-choice' movement began, of course, in disobedience to God in the Garden of Eden.

(We received hundreds of phone calls, threatening to torch our clinic & to kill the 'murdering whores' who worked there.)

Braude's *Radical Spirits* is turned against itself with just enough willingness to read her closely and just enough spite to interpret her badly:

> *These trance speakers, we are told, became the first large group of American women to speak in public. Indeed, it is said that these female spiritualists – who were in opposition to established religion (Christianity) – 'became the only religious sect to embrace women's rights as a first priority', advocating, among other things, the female vote, dress reform, marriage reform, 'free love', socialism, the abolition of slavery, vegetarianism and anti-Sabbatarianism.*

(In 2008, Dr. Tiller was murdered in his own church, again by a 'pro-lifer'. The goal was to scare other doctors who perform abortions.)

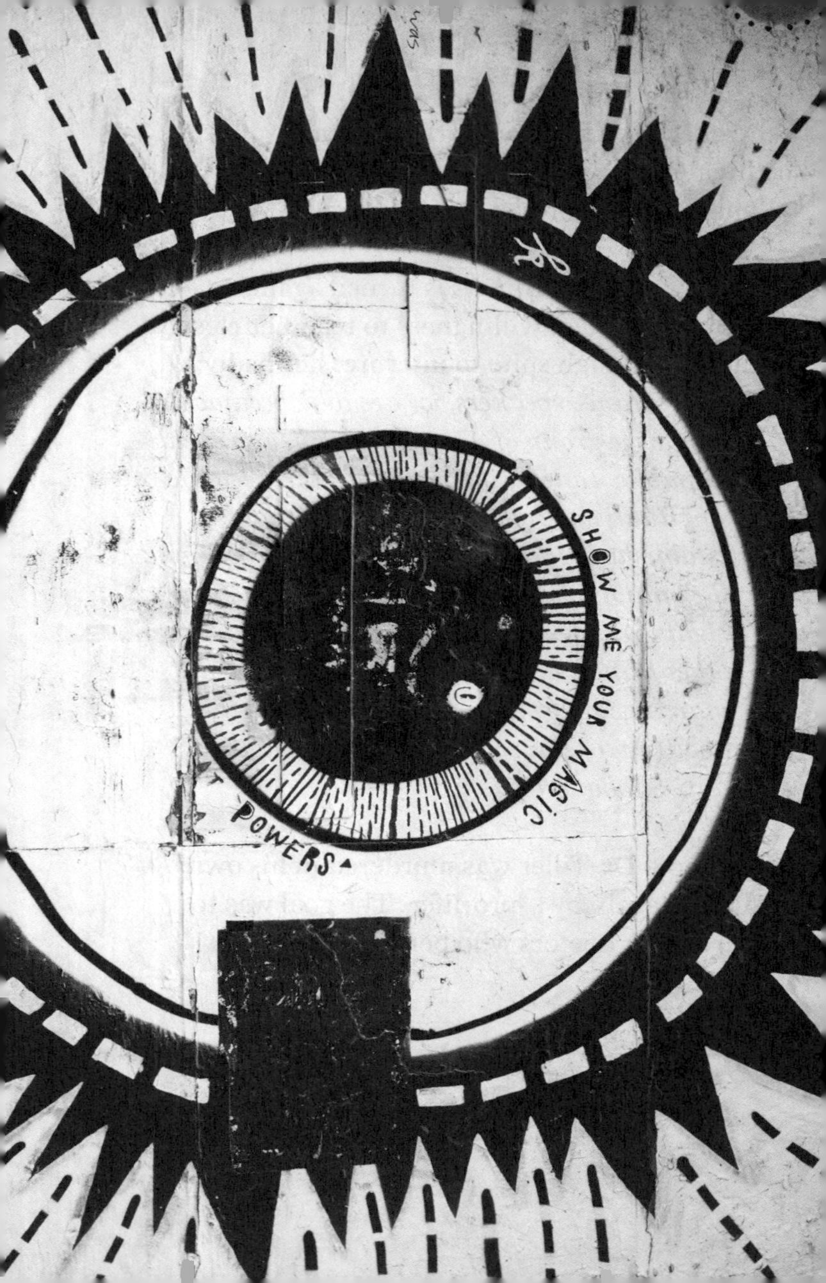
SHOW ME YOUR MAGIC
POWERS

March

I'm in Dublin early on a Sunday morning, meandering through Temple Bar before heading to the airport. I've already rifled through the Secret Book Shop and FreeBird records on Wicklow Street, and then, with a mixture of scorn and curiosity, I've stared at the vacuum-packed metallic pouches lining the shelves of Le Palais des Thés nearby. Tea in the space age.

In the square at Temple Bar the market is just beginning to open. Most of the stalls are still shrouded in old tarpaulins but towards the side there's a small red booth with its curtain partly drawn back. A sign on the ground says 'Turlough Browne. Weekend Special – tarot reading 20 euros'. An hour to kill before checking in for the flight and I have 20 euros. Give it a go.

The booth is tiny – partitioned inside to create a cell beyond the entrance. A tall, broad shouldered man is squashed into the cubicle, sitting on a small chair, almost filling the space. He's wearing an old black suit and he's staring at a pack of cards in his hand. When he sees me he rises uncomfortably and gestures towards a stool that just about fits against the entrance curtain. Sitting down again he sweeps smooth a rough piece of velvet on a little table between us and places the cards on it.

Neither of us speaks. He taps the pack of cards tentatively: his fingers are long and delicate. For a long beat he says nothing.

'A reading then. Is that what you need?', he says and I nod in agreement. 'What's your name?'

I tell him and I ask how him he came to be a tarot reader.

'I always spoke to the dead as a child. That was just normal to me but my parents told me I was a liar. I was always in trouble too so eventually they sent me to a special school in Dublin and I had it all beaten out of me there or so they thought. But when I was seventeen I came here, to the market, and met a woman called Rosemary Parnell. She was fairly old by then but she was still reading the cards and I asked her to take me on and teach me, which she did over the space of a year or two.'

He paused and then started to shuffle the deck on the table.

'I work with my own pack – I based it on the tarot de Marseille but I've modified the four suits with Celtic designs.'

He waves towards the cards but they were facing him and he doesn't turn them around for me to peruse. This, it turned out, would be typical of his approach. I never got to see a card clearly or the right way up. He quickly dealt a simple spread of five cards but he had barely looked at it before he began to drop further cards over the first set. He deals them out in a rapid stream, pausing occasionally when he sees something of interest, never looking to me for a response to the confusion of images.

'The next two years are not easy... A bumpy ride.'

Now he looks at me as if I know what he is referring to and will confirm his statement. I nod, to my initial surprise.

'You'll not find that easy at all but then...' he deals more cards one on top of the other on the growing pile in the middle if the table and stops to ponder what he sees. '... then there's a lot of satisfaction. Francis, everything you've been working for comes right.'

That look again. I nod again. We know what he means.

*

A week later and my mind is still swimming in the stream of cards and images in the Dublin booth. I clear the kitchen table and bring out my Rider Waite tarot pack. I deal five cards, one each for the present, past, and future, one to explore the reason for my question and a final card to assess the potential in the situation.

THE PRESENT: THE FOUR OF WANDS

This is good – it's thought to be one of the best cards in the pack. The four wands are planted on a flat foreground and linked by rose garlands strung high between them. A bridge on the right leads us back towards the walls of a city. Two women are approaching bearing fruit and flowers while others are still busy with preparations behind them. Certainly a celebration, maybe a wedding feast.

The card is dominated by a yellow wash of sunlight, punctuated by red-topped towers in the city walls. The presence of a city is something that reveals the process of making this tarot pack. Arthur Edward Waite, a member of the Golden Dawn in London, devised the set and wrote the initial descriptions and interpretations of each card. But it was Pamela Colman Smith, an artist and fellow member of the Golden Dawn, who painted the images. Comparing Waite's commentaries with the completed images, it's clear that Smith deviated considerably at times, elaborating a tarot within the tarot.

The first edition was published in 1910 and it's grown to be one of the most popular decks since then, probably the 'classic' tarot for most people. Its success lies in the imaginative world created by Colman Smith. While she follows the emblematic designs common to the major arcana cards – Death, The Tower, The Hanged Man etc. – her real innovation lies in the elaboration of a graphic narrative world across the minor cards. With no historical precedents, Colman Smith had free rein to interpret each number in the suits (wands, cups, swords and pentacles) and what she created resembles selected frames from a graphic novel. Her style was ideal for narrative images. Mostly her cards contain the germ of a larger story, but each card stands alone. A particular landscape is common to them – a 'world' as easy to map out as Tolkien's Middle Earth or Iain M. Banks' Culture. But

Colman Smith only hints at wider narratives, scattering suggestive clues throughout the suits. At the same time, she generates enough ruptures to ensure that any attempt at a grand overview is thwarted. In this unfinished world it's the reader's imagination that fills the vacuum and the stories we tell around these images reveal much about us.

THE PAST: THE HERMIT

What has been already. It doesn't take much effort to see that aspect of my life. I live in a house teeming with books, albums and hoarded arcana. Even the lights have burnt out, the odd battery lamp and reading light mark routes through the labyrinth and gas meter men looked scared when they enter. The phone is past repair and the television long gone. One radio survives near the bath, waiting for a Bond assassin to appear while I float oblivious. The kitchen cupboards have been bare for years, I know I have no mice because they would have no means of survival in this wasteland. The chrome sink is a rusty brown from developer, stop and fix while the chemicals themselves are stored on top of a now extinct ceramic hob.

The hermit then: 'closed off' some readers would say, shunning society. But that would be a disservice to this character who, after all, is the only tarot figure to make it onto a Led Zeppelin album cover (their fourth, the inside cover, drawn by 'Barrington Colby MOM', which is believed to be an alias for Jimmy Page). The band link the Hermit to the British legend of the black dog and, inevitably, if you hold the cover up to a mirror the full dog is revealed.

THE FUTURE: THE QUEEN OF WANDS

The Wands represent aspects of energy, fire, positivity and the Queen of Wands is the strongest of the four queens in the Tarot pack. She is the summer, a solar deity who brings life to the desert around her. She is sexuality, sitting frankly with open legs under flowing robes. Her throne is embroidered with sunflowers and rampant lions, there are rocks to her left and mountains in the distance to her right. Her crown is decked with greenery, her robes are golden and she holds a large sunflower in her left hand, and wields a sprouting wand in her right. The throne is flanked with golden lion effigies, but most startling of all is a small black cat that seems to guard her, defiantly staring out at us.

The cat is strange because it has crept in from another world. It feels real compared to the intensely symbolic landscape is sits in. It is also drawn slightly differently, in a more comic mode. This desert cat is a John the Baptist to Krazy and Ignatz who would appear three years later in George Herriman's *Krazy Kat* cartoon strip.

Pamela Colman Smith was often a harbinger of things to come. In New York she was the first painter to be shown in Alfred Stieglitz's Little Galleries of the Photo-Secession (later known as 291) and in London she illustrated Bram Stoker's *Lair of the White Worm* and later joined the Suffragette Atelier, a collective of professional women illustrators working to support the movement for votes for women and sexual equality. As a child she had spent the first ten years of her life in Manchester, at the time a hotbed of spiritualism. Her family moved then to Jamaica where the local folklore made a lifelong impact on her work (she would go on to publish a book of Anancy stories and perform Caribbean ballads at one of her New York openings). In 1901 she was introduced into the Hermetic Order of the Golden Dawn by the Irish poet W.B. Yeats and gradually she rose through the ranks. History may tend to present these esoteric lodges as sedate coteries of spiritual dabbling, but in reality they were raucous and edgy, with disputes spilling into action, such as the attempt by Aleister Crowley to occupy the Vault of Rosenkreutz, a splinter group temple on Blythe Road in London.

THE REASON BEHIND THE QUESTION: TEN OF SWORDS

It is impossible to speak of the ten of swords without noting, fatuously, that it follows the nine of swords. The nine, one of the most nightmarish cards in the pack, has a subtlety that the ten certainly lacks. Ten, in a suit that dwells on the intellect, presents us with a male corpse virtually pinned to the ground by swords in his back from buttocks to the nape of the neck. The sky is a black oil slick, with just a hint of dawn on the horizon. There are only a handful of cards in the tarot that share this darkness: the Devil, the Tower, and the aforementioned nine of swords, of course, which is unremittingly black.

If there is any consolation, it lies in the yellow breach of dawn. The night of violence is coming to an end as the sun rises. And the scene we see should be horrific – a body pierced by ten swords.

But something rings false in this card. The ten protests too much – that many swords in one man's back is faintly ridiculous, the embodiment of overkill. And when we look more closely, the corpse's right hand is fixed in a gesture of blessing. There's a hint of hypochondria in it all, a lapse into theatrical self-pity and self-regard.

THE POTENTIAL WITHIN THE SITUATION: THE QUEEN OF CUPS

A second queen, this one enthroned at the edge of an ocean. She is all sinuous lines, flowing boundaries between rock, sea and regal body. A scallop shell tops her throne, carved undines and mermaids seem alive amid the decor, and her cloak cascades to the sands at her feet where it melds with the pebbles and shells. In this metamorphic landscape, the queen sits oblivious, staring intently at a closed cup she holds before her. The sealed vessel is a mystery. Architectural in form, it resembles a miniature Renaissance church flanked by two ornate sickle-like handles, often described as angels with flared wings.

This seems to be the perfect image of potential – a vessel pregnant with meaning. Add it to the solar dimension of the Queen of Cups: my heliotropic future.

I know it's a good reading but I'm restless. It only gives me a few cards. I want more story. I suddenly understand the Dublin reader's method – the quick-fire dealing of one card after another, one scene after another in a cinematic stream of pure prophecy, writing a script through the random access of cards – the five of pentacles: two paupers limping through snow beneath a glowing stained-glass window; the six of swords: a cloaked woman and child crossing a river, the Styx; two of wands: a man holding planet Earth no bigger than a basketball; Strength: a woman holding open the jaws of a red lion; the tower in smithereens: lightning bolts cleaving the night sky; a blindfolded girl at the seashore wielding two crossed swords; a radiant man hung by one foot like a Zen dancer; the devil with chained sybarites; nightmares with nines; infinity – the lemniscate – suspended above the magician; death's black armour: treading corpses; bandaged wands/men; bondaged swords/women; a cobbler carving pentacles; a lady with a hawk on her wrist; wolf numbers: to measure sun spots; retinal sunflower burst...

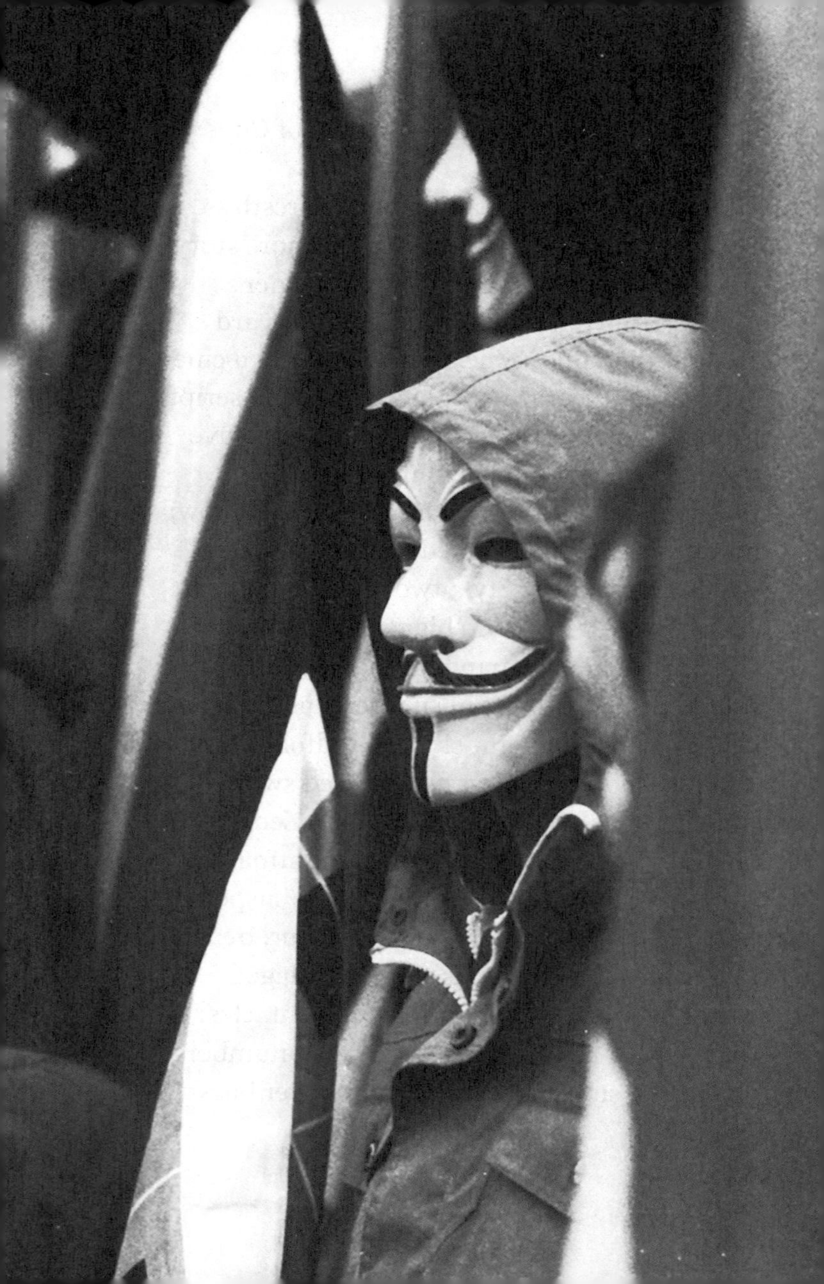

April

‘I killed someone a long time ago.’

‘Seriously? What makes you think you did this?’

‘Nothing “makes me think I did ”, and I didn’t *do* anything. What I mean is, the person was already dying and I left them to it. But it was a decision – I could have saved them.’

‘And why are you telling me this now?’

‘Maybe it’s best to bury these things in something bigger? But it’s good to let it out, get it off my chest.’

‘The something bigger...?’

‘Well, something more varied. Lose it among a multitude of issues blah, blah...’

‘Like hearing voices.’

‘No. Like talking to the fucking dead.’

‘And have you spoken to the person you say you killed? Or have they contacted you’

‘No.’

‘What about the anger you mentioned in the last session? You talked about frequent spells of rage – “like bad weather in your head”, that’s how you described it’

‘So?’

‘Is it related to this death you’ve just mentioned? Does it make you wish for other people’s death? If they annoy you, for instance?

‘Are you really listening? I wasn’t talking about wishing anything. Fuck. I was talking about what actually happened.’

‘Are you angry now?’

‘It was a stupid question. I’m just disappointed in you.’

‘Are you aware that you’re swearing a lot? That can be taken as a form of low-level violence, shoring up insecurities or voicing a frustration at not being able to articulate a point. But you, of all people, can articulate any point you want, very precisely.’

‘Maybe this is pointless.’

‘Well, let’s discuss it then. Who did you kill...?’

I stare at a thermostat attached to the wall just above the skirting board. It’s an old model, simple, not wired into the world.

Remember what they taught you. Focus continuously on one thing, study it in detail until it blocks out external stimuli. Every object has infinite possibilities: unravel them slowly, comprehensively, until you are aware that the question has passed. Then choose to re-join the conversation or remain with the object until you are dismissed.

*

What can I tell you? *Cape Cod girls they got no combs, they brush their hair with codfish bones.* Space is an ocean and this ship is listing. I can hear faint screams in the distance. The metal hull is straining, bulwarks buckling under the pressure of the vacuum around them. Steam pipes are clanking but does a ship like this even run on steam? Time is moving backwards.

*

Humans exist within very narrow bands of sensation. The full range of human hearing extends from 20 to 20,000 hertz. A typical human eye will respond to wavelengths from about 390 to 700 nanometres. The human body can only remain alive within the extremes of 46 F and 115 F and generally hovers around 98.6 F. Our senses seem designed to filter information out rather than to let it in. In a world of mega spawning digital info ballooning we sit tight, resisting the deluge, gripping the sides of our chairs as it rains down upon us.

*

It's the dogwatch and I can use it to think things through. I am putting this down on paper in case there is an attack or in some other way I disappear. To even mention an attack appears pointless now. The Cylons have left us alone for months and our mission to find Earth seems over. The captain is drowning in his cups and his XO has been Johnny Whiskey for centuries. That last jump near killed the Galactica. We're mostly intact – the engines, life support. But there's red lines through her lateral structural members. She's broken her back. She'll never jump again. So we spiral endlessly through the heavens and, somewhere in the bowels of this crate, engine pistons are still booming.

Frack.

When I found my body – Kara's body – in the wreckage of the viper, Leoben turned away in fear. What am I, if she is dead? Even the Cylon was terrified and he had foreseen my future.

I was never more alive. I remember wrapping the remains in a parachute shawl and incinerating the body on a funeral pyre.

(We'll drop her down to the depths of the sea, we'll sing her down with a long, long roll, where the sharks'll have her body and the devil have her soul.)

And then I went back to the ship, the ocean flowing backwards, stars stretched out across space and the crew backing away from me when I stepped off the barge.

*

In 1979, when the American computer scientist John McCarthy began to consider how thermostats think, he told this story:

> *Recently it was too hot upstairs, and the question arose as to whether the upstairs thermostat mistakenly believed it was too cold upstairs or whether the furnace thermostat mistakenly believed the water was too cold. It turned out that neither mistake was made; the downstairs controller tried to turn off the flow of water but couldn't, because the valve was stuck. The plumber came once and found the trouble, and came again when a replacement valve was ordered. Since the services of plumbers are increasingly expensive, and microcomputers are increasingly cheap, one*

is led to design a temperature control system that would know a lot more about the thermal state of the house and its own state of health.

Earlier, McCarthy had already ascribed simple thoughts and beliefs to thermostats. And now, here, he's looking into the future to imagine how those thermostats could evolve: to become more self-conscious.

McCarthy reckoned we would confront such issues in the twenty-first century.

In 2008 Tony Fadell, creator of the iPod, left Apple and in 2010 co-founded Nest Labs in a garage in Palo Alto. The first product he launched was the Nest Learning Thermostat. *Just turn it up and turn it down. The Nest Thermostat learns what temperatures you like and builds a personalised schedule. Teach it efficient temperatures for a few days and, within a week, it'll start setting them on its own.* The machine can be contacted remotely via apps and temperature can be modified from anywhere.

*

Six. Six. Six. Six. Six. Six. Six. Six. Six. Six. Six. Six. Six. Six. Six. Six. Six. Six. Six. Six. Six. Six. Six. Six. Six. Six. Six. Six. Six. Six. Six. Six. Six. Six. Six. Six.

Six. Six. Six. Six. Six. Six. Six. Six. Six. Six. Six. Six. Six. Six. Six. Six. Six. Six. Six. Six. Six. Six. Six. Six. Six. Six. Six. Six. Six. Six. Six. Six. Six. Six. Six. Six. Six. Six. Six. Six. Six. Six. Six. Six. Six. Six. Six. Six. Six. Six. Six. Six. Six. Six. Six. Six. Six. Six. Six. Six. Six. Six. Six. Six. Six. Six. Six. Six. Six. I am numerous. There are twelve Cylon sentient machine models and I am six. To be more precise, I am Caprica Six.

We are cybernetic life-form nodes, followers of the one true god. When we die we simply download into a new identical body and are reborn. There are only twelve models, but there are many copies.

People often confuse me with Head Six. She looks just like me, but she is only visible to Gaius Baltar. I admit I can see her too. But she is one of two angels that appear to me. The other angel resembles Gaius. It's confusing. I know. That is how God works.

*

How to negotiate this transaction?

Small talk. The human-computer symbiosis isn't an epic moment, it's a constant stream of little exchanges.

It's getting cold here, I'm going to increase the temperature. That's fine.

Tomorrow morning I'll heat the water from 6am – it should be good by the time you get up, ready for a bath.

You really know heat, don't you? *Hot and cold, yes.*

Tell me about thermals...

Not now.

*

(At one point if you asked 'what is July 27' Siri would reply that on 27 July 2014 the Gates of Hades will open. Reword the question and she would correct herself and tell you we have been living in hell since May 14, 2005. Prophecy thrives in a bodiless voice.)

Siri may be a harbinger of doom, or a dubious data conflator, but it's possible that she is also the next great medium – allowing messages to flow through to us from a host of machine entities beyond. And as Nest and Siri begin to measure and analyse the environment around them they will also start to pass on messages from nature itself. In *Angels:*

A Modern Myth (1995), Michel Serres describes the all-enveloping system of coded messages already in circulation:

'Each flux breaks down into myriad single particles, but they all go to make up the world. Each of them bears little bits which, when put together, make the larger whole... At any given moment of the day, the breeze plays on your cheek, and since it carries codes from everywhere, it's telling you about the state of the body of the world. If it is able to construct a universe in this way, it follows, conversely, that a universal reason blows in tiny particles...

If winds, currents, glaciers, volcanoes etc., carry subtle messages that are so difficult to read that it takes us absolutely ages trying to decipher them, wouldn't it be appropriate to call them intelligent? What human could ever presume to speak a language that was so precise, refined and exquisitely coded?'

*

Just before sun rising, Mr. Gaeta, with the master at arms, gunner's mate, and Tom Hoshi, seaman, came into my cabin while I was asleep, and seizing me, tied my hands with a cord behind my back, and threatened me with instant death, if I spoke or made the least noise: I, however, called so loud as to alarm everyone; but they had already secured the officers who were not of their party, by placing sentinels at their doors. There were three men at my cabin door, besides the four within; Christian had only a cutlass in his hand, the others had muskets and bayonets. I was hauled out of bed, and forced on deck in my shirt, suffering great pain from the tightness with which they had tied my hands. I demanded the reason of such violence, but received no other answer than threats of instant death, if I did not hold my tongue.

The boat being out, Mr. Hayward and Mr. Hallet, midshipmen, and Mr. Samuel, were ordered into it; upon which I demanded the cause of such an order, and endeavoured to persuade someone to a sense of duty; but it was to no effect: 'Hold your tongue, Sir, or you are dead this instant' was constantly repeated to me.

*

The scientific exploration of data transmission is purely practical and without concern for the quality of the communication. Humans like to command nature rather than open up a dialogue with it. Not only do we want to tell nature what to do, we tend to teach machines to imitate our most competitive traits. McCarthy points out how this has distorted the development of artificial intelligence, using computer chess programs as an example:

> *Alexander Kronrod, a Russian AI researcher, said 'Chess is the Drosophila of AI.' He was making an analogy with geneticists' use of that fruit fly to study inheritance. Playing chess requires certain intellectual mechanisms and not others. Chess programs now play at grandmaster level, but they do it with limited intellectual mechanisms compared to those used by a human chess player, substituting large amounts of computation for understanding. Once we understand these mechanisms better, we can build human-level chess programs that do far less computation than do present programs. Unfortunately, the competitive and commercial aspects of making computers play chess have taken precedence over using chess as a scientific domain. It is as if the geneticists after 1910*

had organized fruit fly races and concentrated their efforts on breeding fruit flies that could win these races.

And so, while scientists observe the thermal death kinetics of fruit flies and, like wayward hothouse parents, compel machines to play better, faster chess, McCarthy suggests that we are missing the real point. Quality time with our machines may be what's needed: to surrender the command line and start a conversation.

*

'I don't understand your theology'

'I think we don't have a theology. We just dance.'

*

Deep in the underbelly of the Internet, machines are now initiating their own dialogues, as they are linked together to create much wider, accurate, systems of information that will form an underlying industrial Internet: energy, transport, health care, and security are already advanced in this process. Perhaps Siri was right: the gates of Hades have opened and we must enter this underworld and beseech Persephone for an ear of corn in silence reaped.

*

'Do you feel guilty?'

A new question. Good one too.

No.

'No.'

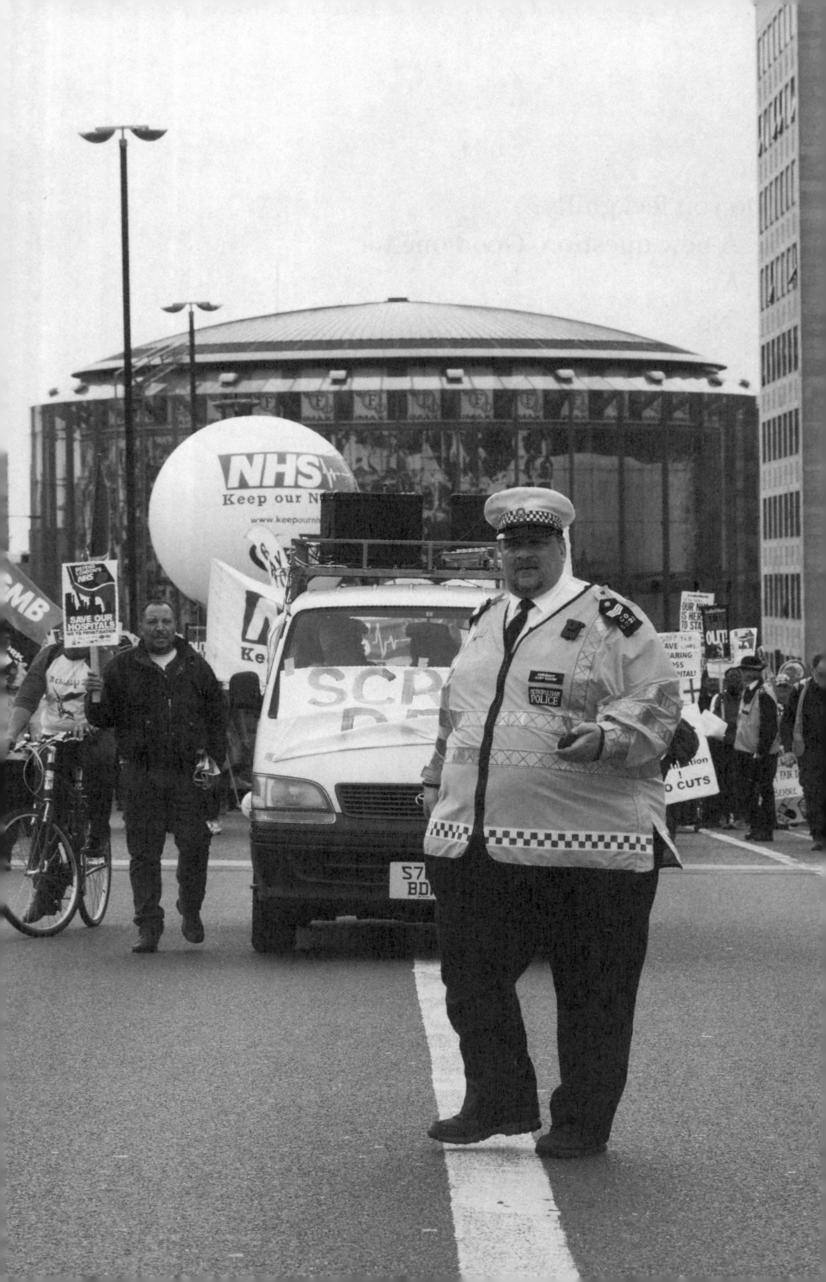
NHS
Keep our N
SAVE OUR HOSPITALS
NO TO PRIVATISATION
POLICE
O CUTS
OUT!

It's a wake until you start walking. Once the corpse is in progress towards a graveyard, then you can call it a funeral.

Under a heavy London sky, behind the Southbank Centre, protesters were gathering for a march against the privatisation and closure of nine accident and emergency departments across London. The scale of what was happening, coming after years of cuts and restructuring, suggested that this was the death rattle of the NHS. Of course something would continue for a few years to come and politicians would pay lip service to it, praising the *wonderful* doctors, the *amazing* nurses and the *long history of achievement* in public health care. But the possibility of accessing that care would continue to recede for most people until it was just a weird uncertain memory.

I'd tried to research the early beginnings of the NHS on the Internet before I went to the protest. The roots were easy: Nye Bevan opening Park Hospital in Manchester seemed to set it all in motion in 1947. But the next great milestone is listed as the discovery of DNA in 1953, and the various histories seem to place that discovery in Cambridge University. I'd known about Rosalind Franklin and how she was marginalised in the story of Crick and Watson, the two (male) scientists who cracked the double helix. Vaguely I knew that Franklin had taken a photo that provided the evidence needed to make the breakthrough. Rosalind Franklin and her PhD student Raymond Gosling, took Photo 51 in the MRC Biophysics Unit on the Strand, three floors down in a basement below the level of the Thames. The Unit was part of King's College London where Franklin was using a process called x-ray crystallography – bombarding crystallised DNA with x-rays to determine the structure of its molecules.

The photograph has a peculiar power. For the non-scientist, the image is banal and illegible. It looks something like a blurry black and white image of a curling stone or a transparent 45 single. On its own terms, it is both spectral and futuristic. The two strands of DNA are unwound and spread in a broad X at the centre of a ghostly circle. It's a first glimpse of human code.

The banners are in primary colours, rainbows of trade union members from Tolpuddle onwards, they must have been made in 1968 or 1969 – the acid splashed years before a retreat to the grainy heroin black and white of the 1970s. Or perhaps they were woven in the ecstasy drenched late 1980s, the concussed aftermath of the miners' strike. It's funny how drugs write history now. Once it was people or events that marked an era, but now it's the dominant chemicals. The pharmaceutical companies tend to reach for authority in their names: Valium, Ativan, Librium, Mogadon, Temazepam. Mobile chemists aim for staccato poetry: 4 dot, toad, red dolphin, Mercedes, bermuda triangles, blue smurfs, dead road, kitty flipping, as, blue ghost, four leaf clover... Both sides know their market and study the zeitgeist.

Suddenly an Irish dancer appears on the front line of the march, dragging a small portable amp behind him like a cabin suitcase. He is a small sinewy man in his late fifties wearing an orange dancing skirt, a bright green waistcoat, woolly hat, orange neckerchief and brogues. The skirt is provocatively short, revealing his bare muscled thighs and it is kept aloft by a large safety pin on the left hand side. I notice a paper Star of David pinned to his stomach. His amplifier pumps out ceilidh music, slicing through the various guitars and communal chants around him. It's disconcerting and ridiculous. No one, though, is tempted to laugh because he is shadowed by a large shaven-headed bouncer in blue ski glasses, toting a large can of Svyturys 1764 and sporting a white T-shirt that proclaims:

HUMANS UNITE
TECHNOLOGY 4 ALL
END MONEY ERA
POL 666.666

Later I realise the front of every major protest is fringed with such characters. The issue at stake in each march is irrelevant to these protesters. The media and the attention gives them a platform for their longer term, eccentric causes. For an instant then, it appears that the protest against the dismantling of the NHS has become a rainbow coalition of conspiracy theorists.

Gradually though the core of the march assembles itself. It's not a simple matter. There are so many layers. Style is vital (and overlooked by anthropologists, sociologists and everyone else who should be paying attention). No one is dressed accidentally. This is a public performance. There is a wide variety of headwear, not just vendetta masks and hoods, but top hats, venetian bird feathers and eye masks, 1960s Dylan caps, flat caps, red berets, clown wigs, Sunday-best Caribbean hats, an infinite variety of hats.

Then there is the full ensemble, often with a retro touch on an English march – anti-apartheid T-shirts, some punk regalia, two-tone suits, skinny ties and pork-pie hats, superman T-shirts with cut-off jeans, army greatcoats, full black tie. Subcultures seem scarce in London after the 1980s, but they still exist as a living spectrum on any given march. This is important. The range of protest histories represented by these fashions creates a sense of continuity, matched by the range of ages visible among the protesters. It's not as if the marchers dress like this every day: their subcultural genres have become costume statements delineating the multi-dimensional facets of their solidarity.

Badges are the minutiae of this phenomenon.

Any given participant, sporting say twenty badges, carries forward each of those histories in the lightest of ways. The badges function as footnotes to be quickly scanned by the viewer or as a personal genealogy of the wearer's radical evolution. On one weathered, middle-aged man they look like campaign medals.

And the music. Someone has rapidly set up a mobile sound system on the back approach to the Southbank Centre and reggae pours down the concrete steps like dub molasses. Soon, though, the microphone is handed out to anyone wanting to rally the marchers. It's a therapeutic process rather than a recruitment tool: everyone there already supports the cause and knows the facts. But the shock and frustration still bursts from each protestor who takes the microphone and the applause seems to be a way for everyone to say 'you think you are alone but it's ok, this is something many people feel'. Almost every speaker finds themselves being hugged by other protesters when they finish. It could be a baptism.

A folk singer. His guitar has stickers for Finchley & Barnet Miners Support Group ('Dig Deep for the Miners', 'Coal Not Dole').

At the far end of Concert Hall Approach, where the front line of the march is coming together, the Strawberry Thieves Socialist Choir stand in readiness. There's only three of them so far, all in red T-shirts with a repertoire prepared and a fruit red banner surrounding a William Morris design. Morris based it on the thrushes at Kelmscott Manor, regular thieves of the strawberries in his kitchen garden.

Then a red wave: dozens of Unite union members make their way to the front, dwarfed by giant round dirigibles, each the size of a large van. They struggle to control them. Four large men are pulling on mooring ropes while the vast red globes bob in the wind above them.

A whistle blasts and the walk begins. We veer left towards Waterloo Bridge, skirting the Franklin Wilkins Building, named after their groundbreaking work on DNA. The march is taken at a brisk pace, as if we're in a hurry to get somewhere. Once on the bridge a large rotund policeman takes pole position, urging the accelerating marchers to catch up behind him. His yellow high-vis jacket barely covers his bulk, which is emphasised by the line of union blimps floating above him. Facing the policeman, the photographers walk backwards across the bridge clicking constantly. Beyond them the fringe protesters lead the way with the sounds of Denis Murphy's 'The Star Above the Garter' drifting back across this surreal parade.

Onlookers fill the brutalist concrete steps that flank the south side of the bridge. They wave, but there's an oppressive air to the scene. Grey clouds push down and rain starts to spit from the sky. Suddenly, from the pavement an undertaker dashes past the march, followed by pallbearers carrying a black draped coffin: the death of the NHS. Insect thin, black feathers curling from his top hat, sailing forwards under a black umbrella, the undertaker pulls ahead of the marchers and the policeman. The photographers swarm around the fast moving tableau until finally a film crew bring them to a halt and start an interview. The unhappy policeman forces them to the side and continues at a canter across the bridge.

I move ahead of the pack to Lancaster Place just off the bridge. There's an interesting scenario developing: a young couple are sitting in the middle of the road with two large Siberian huskies and the police have withdrawn further up the street, leaving them all in peace. The dogs are serene, Buddha-like in their friendliness and capacity to ignore the fringe of chaos around them. The large policeman and his blimp army are heading towards them at a clip. Photographers have slowed and many are now sitting on the road taking shots of this odd sanctuary. There's something about those dogs and their owners that is a little Woodstock, the nearest we've come to a utopian moment.

Before the main body of the march can arrive, the police move in and gently prompt everyone to get up. The coffin has fallen back into the mass of the church and now the leading figure is a small woman, bird-like, nested in a wheelchair, wrapped in a blue and black synthetic fur coat. There's a paper hat crowning her stern head and she's clutching a regal sceptre topped with three plastic hands that rattle like a castanet. She's quickly overtaken as people pour off the bridge.

The march whips around the corner, and starts moving down the Strand towards Whitehall. Unite have emerged in strength and eclipsed the competition in the home straight. A tall Caribbean woman, Sunday hat and floral blue

Sunday dress, starts to dance. Surrounded by drummers, she spins, crouches, windmills and shimmies down the street: the street where Photo 51 was taken in a subterranean laboratory. The raw blast of sound is amplified as it bounces off the buildings. Photographers race alongside the musicians and retreat as the dancer shoots forwards and then drifts, in a blurred spiral across the front of the parade. This is the moment, the point of release when some unspecified energy rises from the front and runs through the marchers like a spark on a fuse. It's the moment when people are unstoppable, they're ready 'to wrestle the earth from fools' and they pour through the streets down to Whitehall.

But, close to Downing Street there's a bottle-neck. A stage is waiting, tall and narrow, like a gallows. Speeches are already in progress with a reliable rhythm, rhetorically inevitable, always rising to a fist-waving point. It's like hitting a wall: all that energy smashes into the steel barriers and ebbs away like a dead wave. Almost immediately, the unions are packing up their balloons. The eccentric frontrunners are changing out of their costumes into streetwear. People begin to drift back up Whitehall. Energy dissipates.

And after all the stragglers, a green line advances up the street. Cleaners, cleansing carts and hose-washing automated brush trucks sweep past the defeated people. It's hard to avoid the metaphorical dimensions of the process. Everything said and done is being erased, literally wiped from the earth. In the distance, riot police relax and queue at a van for ice cream cones.

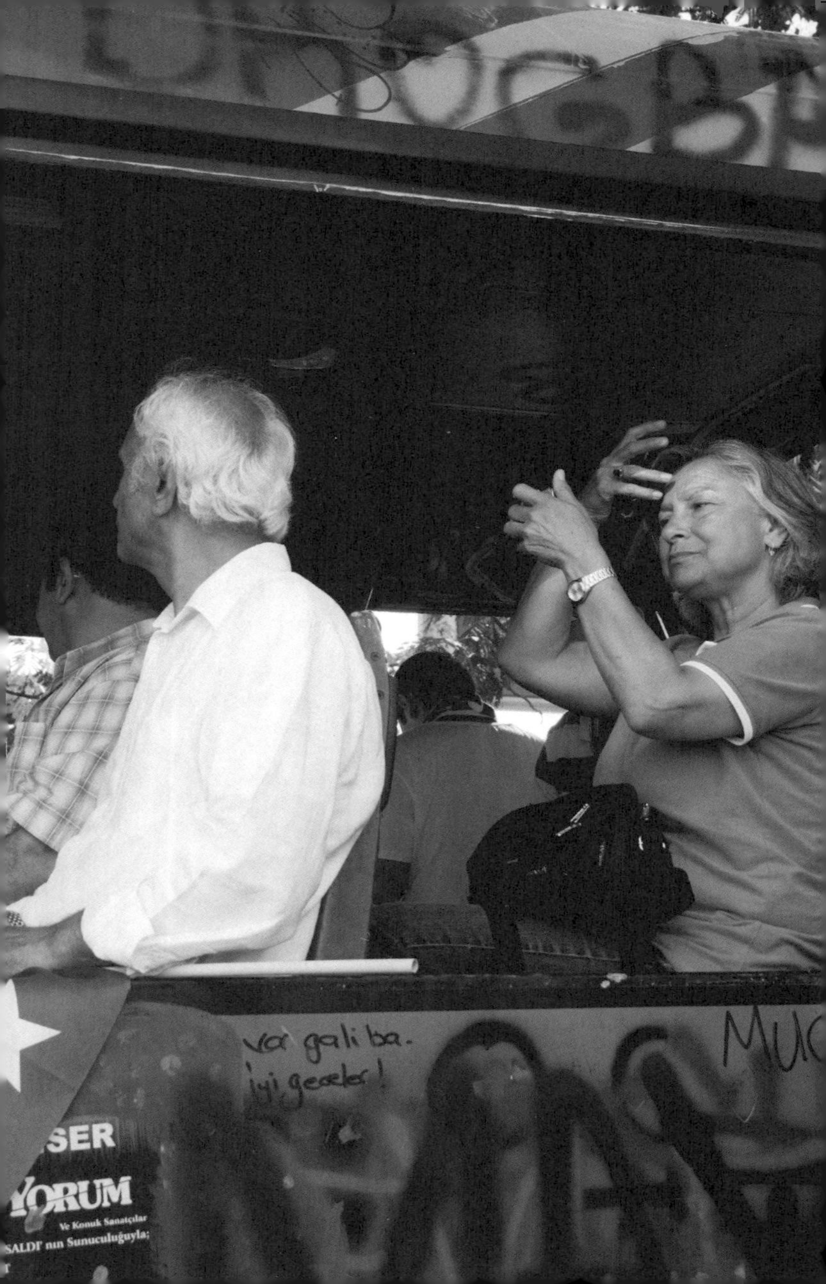
va galiba.
iyi geceler!
MUC
SER
YORUM
Ve Konuk Sanatçılar
SALDI' nın Sunuculuğuyla;

June

Çare Drogba! (The Cure is Drogba!)

8 JUNE

It's taken nearly an hour to get from the airport to the Beyoğlu district and eventually the taxi crawls to a halt in Siraselviler Avenue, just before a makeshift barricade of metal and rubble. We get out and the driver insists on coming with me to the hotel. Suddenly the road is full of people towards us, then there's a siren wailing and the crowd parts to let four people run past us with a man on a stretcher, an oxygen mask pressed to his mouth. The siren is simply a bullhorn and someone is running beside the stretcher with a flashing blue and red light – a homemade ambulance.

A few metres beyond the barricade we're on the edge of Taksim Square. The taxi driver shakes my hand and says goodbye. I fight through a dense crowd of people pressed against the doors of the hotel and climb the steep stairs to the lobby.

There's a sense of emergency everywhere, compounded by the hotel receptionists who are trying to work as if it's business as usual. They're visibly annoyed by the TV crews and their demands. 'What floors have the best Wi-Fi?' 'I need a high-speed connection and a window overlooking the square.' 'Would you like to tell me what you think of the protests? What do you think will happen next?'

No. They would not like to tell anyone what they think about anything at all. They are clearly offended that their city's tourist spots are being ignored, possibly damaged by these people in the street with their hunger for catastrophe. Suddenly a woman in the lobby faints and everyone around shouts for help. A glass of water appears and she comes round. The TV crews ignore her and try to regain the attention of the receptionists who look confused, as if they have found themselves working in an alternative dimension.

I come as a relief to them. I do not have a TV camera, a sound boom or a walkie-talkie. They give me a high room with a view of the square and a fast connection. In the lift on the way up, a man from Northern Ireland with a Fáinne in his lapel tells his film crew to get a shot of him and the crowds from his balcony.

In the calmness of my room I unpack, prepare my camera, check my batteries and head straight down again into the square. Taksim is cut off from the rest of the city. Thousands of people are moving in and out of the park, promenading.

*

On Mete Street, running down the side of Gezi Park, a series of burnt-out buses is blocking the route. Each is colonised by a small crowd – teenagers and men on the roof of each bus waving flags, playing drums, posing for photographs. The sides of the buses have been painted with multi-coloured slogans and draped with makeshift banners. I take a photograph against the sun and light flares through the trees. Time shifts and I am suddenly in front of the Further bus in 1964. Ken Kesey, Neal Cassady and Cathy Casamo waving freak flags from its windows.

Inside the buses something extraordinary is happening. People sit in the skeletal, blackened seats smiling, laughing or just waiting, as if the bus is going somewhere. There are middle-aged couples, young guys, serious girls in hijabs – every bus is full and the anticipation is electric. These people are beginning a journey – it is their metaphor, not mine – I am simply witnessing a bus full of people who know they will not return to the lives they had left that morning...

*

9 JUNE

Strung between two trees there is a sheet filled with a green outlined text that looks embroidered: 'If God gives you tear gas make lemonade.' It must refer to Charles Fourier. No? There's no one to ask. The tents around it are dark and closed, everyone finally asleep for an hour or two before the drums and zurna burst the silence again.

Close to the edge of the park there is a small glass building that never sleeps. Inside a wide television screen is suspended from the ceiling: scattered insomniacs slump in plastic bucket chairs and watch the rolling coverage of their occupation. A middle-aged couple are browsing on an iPad and they offer to google Fourier and lemonade. He is rumpled in a sweater and sweatpants but something about his glasses suggests retired university lecturer. His wife is swathed in a long shawl, similarly academic glasses. Google works and she reads me a quote from Fourier:

'When the human race has extended the cultivation of the globe beyond sixty degrees north, the planet's temperature will be less extreme and generally much more pleasant; the rutting will become more active, the aurora borealis will occur more frequently, will be fixed over the pole and will broaden out into a ring or crown.'

'Rutting?' she says. I shrug.

'Maybe it meant something else then?'

'Could be.'

'Vines will grow on the sixtieth parallel... Warsaw will have groves of orange trees...'

'Where is the sixtieth parallel', he asks.

More Google. Just north of Oslo and just south of Helsinki.' They both laugh.

'That's north.'

A long scroll, a quiet moment, and she finds the lemonade, reading slowly.

'The crown's influence will change the taste of the sea and disperse or precipitate bituminous particles by spreading a *boreal citric acid*. In combination with salt, this liquid will give the sea a flavour of the kind of lemonade known as *aigresel*. It will be easy to remove the saline and citric particles from the water and render it drinkable, which will make it unnecessary for ships to be provisioned with barrels of water.'

'What is aigresel?'

'It's the mixture of citric acid and salt... that's a sour lemonade.'

'But why is it easier to remove salt from the lemonade than from normal sea water? I don't understand...'

'It's utopian.'

They smile.

'It's lemonade.' He says. 'So yes, I agree. It's a utopia. And good for the eyes after tear gas if you take out the salt...'

'Wait!' she says as I get ready to go. She reads again, leaning over the back of her chair, holding her shawl in place with one hand, gripping her iPad with the other.

'God has calculated what would be most suitable, even down to preparing a special position for a capital of universal unity. Even today everybody is struck by the uniquely marvellous way he has made Constantinople', she almost shouts,

'*Constantinople!* – a centre of usefulness and pleasure. Everybody sees the hand of God in it', and says 'This is where the capital of the world should be!'

'We are in utopia!'

*

Going down to the hill to see what the noise is about, the streets dividing and sub-dividing on the descent until finally I'm winding through alleys barely wide enough for two people and a gutter. The noise remains unseen as clouds of dust – no – gas, eye-watering gas, rise up through the buildings and I walk into nothingness and then a baton swifts past my eyes and bounces of the wall. Someone's suddenly pushing from behind so forwards is the only direction, further into the white clouds and then shoved sideways tripping into another alley. Head crunching against the wall as others stampede, lifted roughly by the armpits and rammed into the onrush we are roaring up through billowing plumes metallic clunk of hissing shells falling on stone up towards oxygen screaming blindness eyes boiling and blistering, clattering pots and pans clashing and ricocheting in the narrow alley we are here for you...

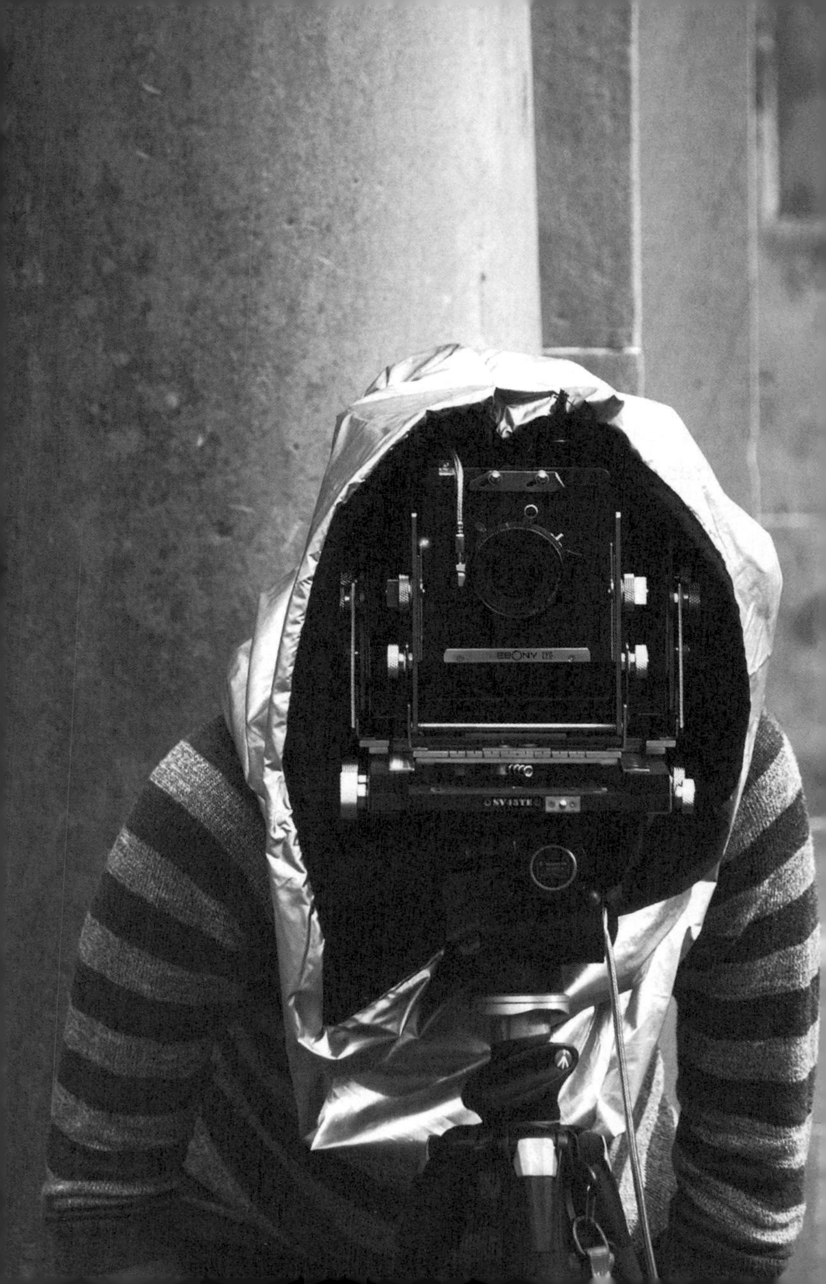
EBONY

July

Sitting in a circle in the basement of the building. A medium talks us into a light trance. Churched and sinking, my metabolism slows to a crawl: time stretches and bends into landscape. I spindle and drift, trying not to fall into a deeper trance (something considered inappropriate at these sessions). We've been told this is the point where we may find our spirit guide, an entity that can help us negotiate the many voices likely to surround us. I can't take this seriously. Maybe I'm trying too hard but I seem able to summon a celebrity guide at will: a drawling Gore Vidal one day, a precise Cecil Day Lewis the next. Nothing but my imagination tuning into a nostalgia channel. To make things worse, I get annoyed at the implicit colonialism in the whole guide phenomenon. The best of them, the Sherpas of the underworld, are predictably Chinese or Native American. Of course, in their otherness, they are wise and attuned to many frequencies that more rational Europeans cannot access. Why is it never an earthy Margery

Kempe or Hildegard of Bingen, whistling quietly to herself as she leads me down stone corridors, keys rattling on her belt...

To be fair, none of the other members of the circle are tempted by the lure of empire. The few that have encountered guides have found them to be elderly Glaswegians, gruff but willing to map the territory and point out the sights: spiritual taxi drivers.

Moving reluctantly back to an alert state, I realise that I'd been sitting opposite a large sepia photograph of a Native American Chieftain framed on the wall. That must have kicked off my annoyance with guides... I've never been sure what the status of the photograph is for the current staff of the church. At the entrance to the building there is also a series of classic spiritualist photographs from the nineteenth and early-twentieth centuries. They are almost a greatest hits selection: a woman clutches a table as ectoplasm pours from her mouth; an old couple look sideways at the miasmic appearance of a face in a cloud of mist; a woman sits forlornly while a spectral figure of a man comforts her with a hand on her shoulder; a table tips violently forwards as a speaking horn floats above a disconcerted medium; a woman struggling to contain an intense ribbon of light burning across the gap between her rigid outstretched arms.

I've always been fascinated by these images. They are all clearly fakes: either double exposures or collages devised in the darkroom. The earliest and most famous practitioners in the genre, photographers such as William Mumler and Fred Hudson, were eventually accused of fraud. It's just as important to remember though that they thrived for several years before being denounced. Mumler rose to such fame at one point that he took a photograph of Abraham Lincoln's wife, Mary Todd, with the dead president's spirit watching over her. Even the trial that effectively ruined his life featured the legendary showman P.T. Barnum who accused Mumler of perpetrating a hoax on his clients and the public. There was clearly a hunger for these images and they continued to be produced, reviving alongside spiritualism in the 1920s, fuelled by the waves of post-war grief.

One of Mumler's defenders was Professor James Coates, a 'phrenologist and mesmerist, who has worked up a great reputation in circles outside the spiritual.' Coates was said to live in Glasgow, though in his preface to *Photographing the Invisible* (1911) he gives his address as Glenbeg House, Rothesay. Coates pointed out that scientists were photographing the invisible. He may have found inspiration for that claim in the first X-ray department, founded in Glasgow Royal Infirmary in 1896, after Wilhelm Röntgen asked for Lord Kelvin's support for his new radiation experiments.

The subtitle of Coates' book, however, points to his own particular interests: *Practical Studies in Spirit Photography, Spirit Portraiture, and other Rare but Allied Phenomena.* Science had shown that electricity moved invisibly through the air, that radiation could be captured and used to create images, and that radio waves could transmit sounds across oceans. Coates argued that spirits too were an operative force and it was this attribution of agency that gave his book an edge. Having examined many spirit photographs, he concluded that, yes, they were double exposures or, at times, collages composed of photographs of the deceased superimposed over images of living subjects.

But Coates claims that the uncanny transformations are not the result of actions by the photographer, his subject or any living medium. Instead, the process is actually controlled by the interaction of the camera, the film and whatever invisible force is attempting to communicate through the medium of photography:

> *For every figure, image, portrait, etc., revealed by the process of development, some* unknown cause *has produced a material, chemical change in substance of the film; and through the process of developing, a further chemical change is brought about which is necessary in order to reveal the image or portrait produced by the* unknown factor *or factors.*

This theory was important for several reasons. Most urgently for spirit photographers, Coates' emphasis on the operation of invisible forces shifted attention away from the photographer's manipulation of images through double exposure or collage. It allowed spiritualists to acknowledge that this kind of manipulation was evident and simultaneously rendered it impossible to verify the existence of the 'unknown factors' that may have produced the image.

This whole question of fraud or the operation

of invisible forces, though, is sensational enough to distract from another aspect of the phenomenon that relates more directly to the ontology of photography itself. There has been a long-held and persistent emphasis on the indexical power of the photography in the history of art and visual culture tends to marginalise double exposures, spirit photography and surrealist playfulness. Darkroom tricks are frowned upon in a medium where the relationship with reality is seen as exact.

The photographic historian John Tagg is often cited in discussions of the indexical nature of photography and his works have definitively articulated the ways in which photography's role in repressing 'the deviant body' in society. Tagg has charted the ways in which power has focused on the indexical and used it to define and control various populations (the police building archives of photographs of criminals, Galton and Bertillon for instance, or the psychiatric use of photographs as evidence of an illness). This doesn't mean however that Tagg himself is committed to a realist position in which the photographic image corresponds to an existing reality: 'the indexical nature of the photograph – the causative link between the pre-photographic referent and the sign can... guarantee nothing at the level of meaning'. Tagg, though, uses this conclusion as the basis for an examination of how power then frames photography falsely within the notion of an indexical relationship with the world for its own ends. The ontology of photography is bypassed in his dissection of power.

Other current critiques of photography such as Francois Laruelle's *The Concept of Non-Photography* (2011) do attempt to address the ontology of the photograph, going much further than Tagg to claim that the camera can produce an 'objectivity so radical that it is perhaps no longer an alienation; so horizontal that it loses all intentionality; this thought so blind that it sees perfectly clearly in itself; this semblance so extended that it is no longer an imitation, a tracing, an emanation, a "representation" of what is photographed.' Laruelle unmoors the photograph from its role as a simulacrum of reality: it is no longer evidence but something much more abstract, it is 'fractal' and any part of the photograph can contain all the possibilities of photography.

Reading Laruelle from a photographer's perspective, though, it becomes hard to see why there would be a need to take more than one photograph in any lifetime. The almost total abstraction of the image from its original source in reality and his emphasis on its fractal quality neuters any discussion of the 'subject matter' of the photograph and the possibility of an active role for the image in daily life.

What Laruelle's philosophy lacks is any sense of the physical and social interaction that is often involved in the production of a photograph. In my own experience the process of documenting a protest begins early in the day when I make a final edit of potential lenses and pack them in a bag. Depending on the weather and distance from any event it's still a question of which lens to use in a given situation on the street. Those technical choices fall somewhere between my judgement and Nikon's design decisions: the choices I make are also determined and shaped by their specifications.

It's the social situation that is most important though. The protesters as a group will be trying to sense where I am on the spectrum of support. Am I one of them? A sympathetic outsider? A journalist looking for a sensational image? Or a policeman compiling records...? Then, for any particular image there is either an impulse to take the shot without any mutual acknowledgement or to gain trust and permission. The latter process is a momentary thing: it's a question of eye contact and consent through a quick nod. It's a lightning contract but in certain situations there isn't time for even such an instantaneous negotiation.

On these points Laruelle does not help. Ariella Azoulay, however, is more useful in her ongoing analysis of the social contract in photography:

> *In contradistinction to the assumption that it is possible to discuss photography only from the point of view of its product and to attribute to the photographer sole rights over it, I claim that photography is a product resulting from the actions of many agents and that the photograph is only a sample of the relations between people or an effect of the space of relations between them.*

That feels true to the experience of taking a photograph in a protest situation. What's most important though is that she takes this further, describing the interaction in 'the space of relations' as political:

> *In contradistinction to the assumption that 'the political' is an attribute that may characterise one image and may be absent from another, I use the term 'political' to describe a space of relations between people who are exposed to one another in public, and I analyse photography, rather than the individual photograph as one of the manifestations of this space...*
>
> *The co-presence of individuals at the time that the photograph is taken is admittedly usually managed in accordance with the ritual of photography, but it is never totally subordinated to the latter. The space that extends between them and the spectators of their photograph, is a political space where human beings look at one another, speak and act in a manner that is not solely subordinate to disciplinary constraints, nor to ones of governance.*

The most optimistic element of Azoulay's ontology is this final point in which she defines the whole process as something resistant to authority. She goes on to argue that this ungovernable space remains open as the viewer of the photograph continues to redefine it and unravel any sense of fixity.

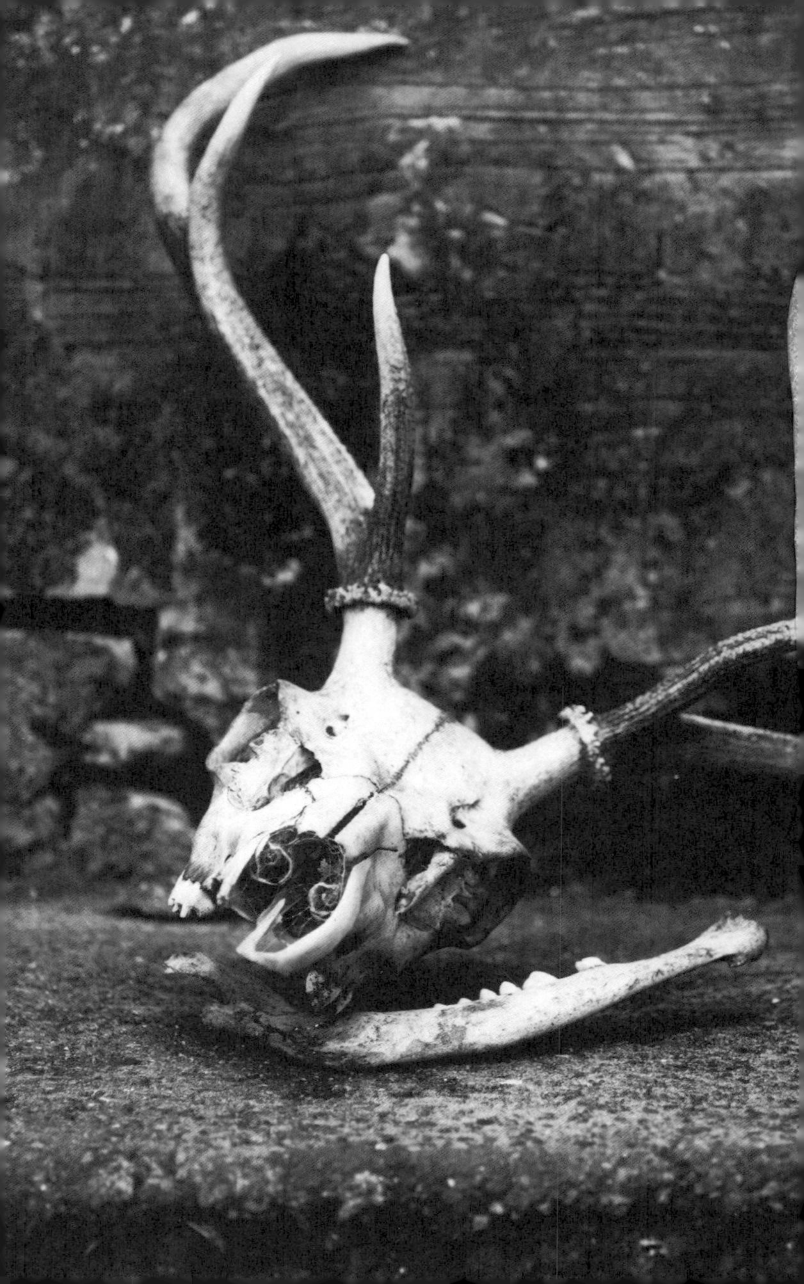

August

11 AUGUST

There was a wine-dark bruise on my left arm and I couldn't explain it. The bus pushed north while Sue patiently explained Sufi theology. I fell asleep and when I woke up we were in Fort William. Passengers hunched against the walls of Morrisons supermarket and hikers wandered aimlessly up and down the endless main street. The town turned out to be a crossing place. The rest of the journey pulled us deep into a green world, lush and strange, pollen heavy.

From a pier beyond Portree a ferry ushered us out from Skye, watched over by the Cuillin as we woozily aimed for Raasay. Crows on the dock wall watched as we disembarked. Rain spattered across the windscreen of the minibus that took us to Raasay House.

My room was dark and secluded, high above a bright, overflowing garden, looking out onto the forest trees bordering the grounds. The stillness was a relief after the long bus trip.

Something flitting across the mirror shocked me. I'd fallen asleep and just woken not knowing where I was, swimming in the shadows of the room, surfacing suddenly and realising I'd be late for the group dinner.

12 AUGUST

A medievalist. Professor Clare Lees, is explaining to us that Columba and his monks were heavily influenced by the desert fathers – early Christians who retreated to the Scetes desert in Egypt to live as hermits or in monasteries. Rejecting all luxury they dwelt in the utmost simplicity, their lives shaped by the discipline of monastic routine or by solitary prayer and meditation. Iona was founded on similar principles. The Atlantic ocean became the desert of the western monks and the islands of the Hebrides were retreats from the mainland. Columba's bio-grapher, Adamnan, mentions one monk, Cormac, who 'sailed too far' and encountered swarms of loathsome insects striking the keel and sides of the curragh so violently they threatened to penetrate the leather skin of the vessel.

Cormac had set off to find a 'desert in the pathless sea'. Perhaps the islands of the Hebrides were too tightly bound to the edge of the continent. Imagine listening to the language of rain and praying directly to the face of God. Your senses would be so heightened that the fact of a living, breathing being, on the next island, could be corrosive.

Pack provisions and flee.

*

Each monk hunkered in his beehive, on wet flagstones, plumping pollen behind his knees. They are cleaning their wings with their forelegs, buzzing and scraping around their cells. Across the Hebrides there is an electrostatic crackle in the atmosphere, the sum of prayers aimed at rainclouds.

Living every day in the shadow of the apocalypse. Clouds roll in across the vast expanse of silver water, crashing on the shoreline. These monks, they dream of John of Patmos, burrowing deep in his cave on that island, stepping off the edge of reason, falling from orbit, burning up in the flames of revelation. I hear behind me a voice saying, I am Alpha and Omega, the first and the last and I turn. His head and his hair are white like wool, as white as snow; and his eyes are a flame of fire. And he has in his right hand seven stars: and out of his mouth is a sharp two-edged sword: he blazes like the fiery sun.

'I lived, and was dead; and, behold, I am alive for evermore.'

13 AUGUST

Roland Barthes, in *How to Live Together*, contrasts the cenobitic impulse, the disciplined rhythm of communal life in a monastery, with the idiorrhythmy of monks living as hermits. Both movements were born in the Egyptian desert; both provided models for the monks of Iona and the Hebrides. It was, Barthes concludes, a question of power:

> *Once again, what we're dealing with is: a consubstantial relationship between power and rhythm. Before anything else, the first thing that power imposes is a rhythm (to everything: a rhythm of life, of time, of thought, of speech). The demand for idiorrhythmy is always made in opposition to power... idiorrhythmy: a means of safeguarding rhuthmos, that is to say a flexible, free, mobile rhythm; a transitory, fleeting form, but a form nonetheless.*

*

Vikings 793. Shut up or get cut up. Dragons appear and terrorise the North. The Boneless Brothers hit the South. Ram raids in Iona and Lindisfarne. Then payback: trade, technology, crafts and theology. Another apocalypse: the world goes down. Yggdrasil shivers when Hel bursts open. Garn the wolf runs free. The sun turns black and flames scorch the sky. The dark dragon harvests the dead.

14 AUGUST

I'm reading Thomas Merton's final journals from the 1960s. He was a beat poet and Trappist monk who drew Western Christianity closer to Zen Buddhism. In his journals, Merton struggles constantly with the issue of monastic retreat in the wake of the Cuban missile crisis and escalating involvement in Vietnam. One journal entry cuts to the quick of the matter:

The stupidity and blindness of American power, which, in its own terms is perfectly 'logical' – and yet its terms are fantastically arbitrary and respond only to the 'reality' of a thinking that goes on within an artificial and closed system. To defend your own reality and then impose it forcefully on the outside world is paranoia.

At the same time he berates himself just as harshly – 'Solitude and dissent become more and more impossible, more and more absurd.'

He finds himself censored by the church authorities and persists in smuggling various protest articles out to the underground press. Paradoxically he retreats into even greater solitude seeking permission to live in a hermitage – a cinder block building in the woods of Gethsemani Monastery, Kentucky. There, he practises listening to the natural world around him. He was several years ahead of the countercultural retreat to the land and he foresaw the tsunami of consumerism earlier than most ('The time will come when they will sell you even your rain.')

Nature speaks to Merton in a pure, paradisiacal language:

The rain I am in is not like the rain of cities. It fills the woods with an immense and confused sound. It covers the flat roof of the cabin and its porch with inconsistent and controlled rhythms. And I listen, because it reminds me again and again that the whole world runs by rhythms I have not yet learned to recognize, rhythms that are not those of 'the engineer'.

What a thing it is to sit absolutely alone, in the forest, at night, cherished by this wonderful, unintelligible, perfectly innocent speech, the most comforting speech in the world, the talk that rain makes by itself all over the ridges, and the talk of the watercourses everywhere in the hollows!

Nobody started it, nobody is going to stop it. It will talk as long as it wants, this rain. As long as it talks I am going to listen.

Out here, on the periphery, Merton is immaculate. Reading by lamplight:

My Coleman lantern. Beautiful lamp: It burns white gas and sings viciously but gives out a splendid green light in which I read Philoxenos, a sixth-century Syrian hermit...

Philoxenos in his ninth memra *(on poverty) to dwellers in solitude, says that there is no explanation and no justification for the solitary life, since it is without a law. To be contemp-lative is therefore to be an outlaw. As was Christ. As was Paul.*

One who is not 'alone', says Philoxenos, has not discovered his identity. He seems to be alone, perhaps, for he experiences himself as 'individual'. But because he is willingly enclosed and limited by the laws and illusions of collective existence, he has no more identity than an unborn child in the womb. He is not yet conscious. He is alien to his own truth. He has senses, but he cannot use them. He has life, but not identity. To have an identity, he has to be awake, and aware. But to be awake, he has to accept vulnerability and death. Not for their own sake: not out of stoicism or despair – only for the sake of the invulnerable inner reality which we cannot recognise (which we can only be) but to which we awaken only when we see the unreality of our vulnerable shell. The discovery of this inner self is an act and affirmation of solitude.

15 AUGUST

We head for Hallaig, tramping through ferns as high as our heads and up hills studded with thistles. We are rewarded by a view across the sea that is Homeric in its scope. Behind us, the buried walls of the village and the history of the clearances. Sorley MacLean has followed us, or at least the spirit of his Raasay drawl, that noise scratched into our brains forever.

The dead have been seen alive. Dark blood flows, spirits rise. The men lie still at the gable of every house. Trees move in the forest at Screapadal. Unwept, unburied, Odysseus shall return through spiteful Neptune and the girls a wood of birch trees standing tall, with their heads bowed. Screapadal. Birch, rowan and hazel. Over dark seas, the lonely whale paths, endless time. The deer.

16 AUGUST

Midnight. I'm kneeling on the floor in the darkness of my room. The laptop flips to full screen and then the sun appears, blistering as it rotates – black and yellow, light flaring out across the room. I can hear voices below, rising from the garden. There is a second sun orbiting in the mirror, looped like the first, reversing its rotation. Sun streaming from the solar and heliospheric observatory across an invisible network to Raasay, beamed through flowers, waves, time, trees, particles and upturned dinghies.

Roland Barthes again – 'mysticism is the atopia of religion'.

Atopia (Greek): without a place.

17 AUGUST

The deluge. A door bangs somewhere in the house, the wind roars through the halls. A weathervane explodes. The idea of a hare praying to a rainbow no longer seems so daft. Words are slipping the leash and the gospel of John suddenly makes sense:

In the beginning was the Word, and the Word was with God, and the Word was God. The same was in the beginning with God. All things were made by him; and without him was not any thing made that was made. In him was life; and the life was the light of men. And the light shineth in darkness; and the darkness comprehended it not.

This is the logic that lies beneath the books illuminated by those early monks. The actual making of the word, its materiality on the page, was a sacred thing. The fantastical animals that live between the hand-drawn letters, writhing across the page, inhabit a kind of heaven.

But the darkness does not disappear. It comprehended not but it remains. There are no clean endings: that gospel is prickly with misunderstandings, a labyrinth of words.

18 AUGUST

Glasgow. I drop my bag in the kitchen. A girl is sitting straight-backed against the far wall, her head bowed.

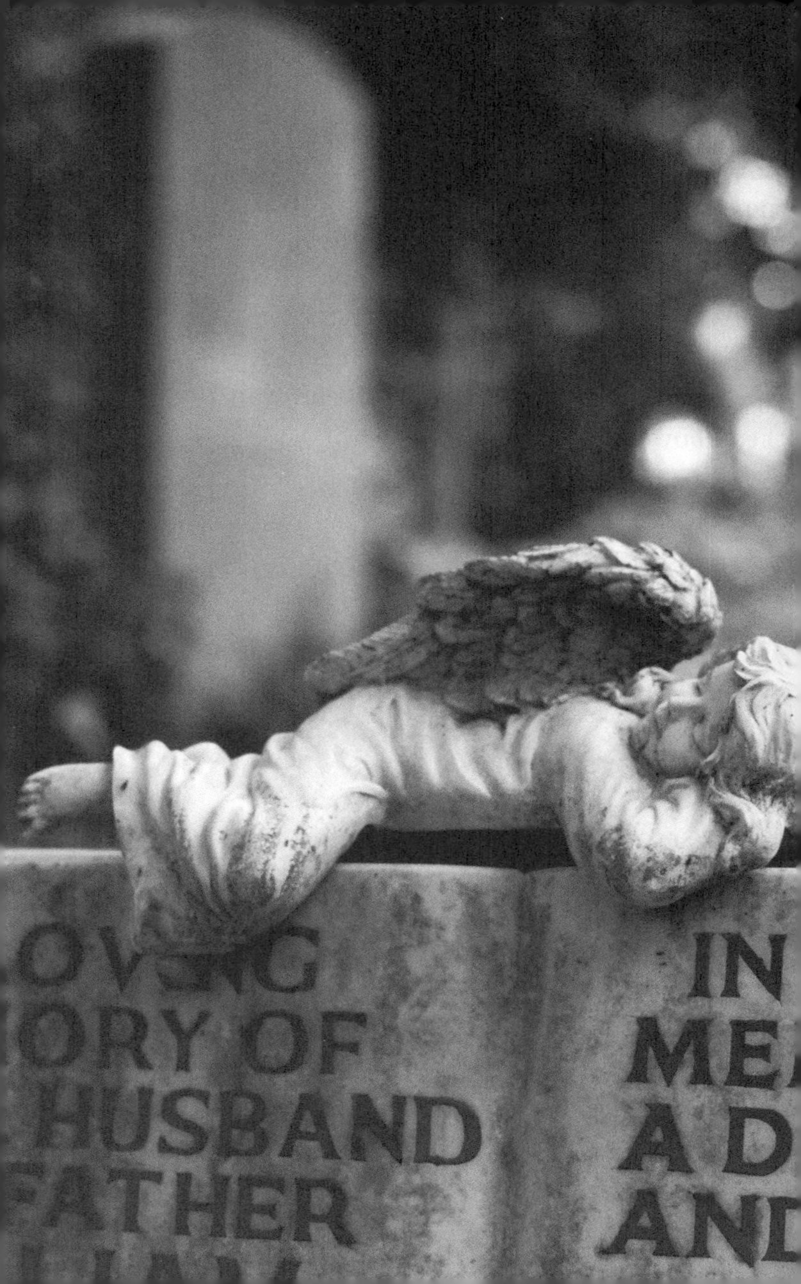
OVING
ORY OF
HUSBAND
ATHER
IN
ME
AD
AND

September

Yesterday, I blacked out. Talking to someone one moment, the next I'm staring at their shoes. Everyone is polite. They help me up, we talk about fever and the flu. But it's not the only symptom. I walk past a circular wall light and there's a burst of distortion in my right ear – a painful cloud of dirty static. It erupts, wipes out all hearing for several metres and then vanishes. There are moving shadows and spots in my peripheral vision.

When I dream, I walk through the streets of a village. Armagh Street. Newry Street. The Square: men spitting on their hands and shaking on a deal; horses restive and edgy between vans and trailers, young boys with switches. The back street and the shambles. The barracks: towers, nets and acres of camouflage; chinooks lifting themselves slowly from the ground like drugged and weary dragonflies.

*

Afternoon. Dust motes streaming across the room. A flea shoots up into the light from the floor. I hear a crack as it takes off like a ricochet. Could it really have made that much sound? It moves in a lazy slow-motion arc through the radiant dust particles like a comet through space debris. More ricochets, more fleas soaring up into the light, curving into a descent to darkness again.

I try to sit up but only succeed in turning my head towards the bookcase where the spines and bindings are smearing into a liquid spill of colours before settling like a shaking jelly. The fleas don't seem to be aiming for me but looking at my bare arms. I can see the flesh is red as a pincushion with tiny multiple bites, a wave of tiny perforations.

I need to wake up – the dizziness is pulling me further into a terrifying darkness – I don't know what I'll find there. I'm worried whether I can deal with what I find there: having a bath seems a way to burn me back to consciousness.

I must have believed that because I wake up naked on the tiled floor of the bathroom. Steam everywhere. The light is now physically twisting in space, spun into braids by the frosted glass of the bathroom windows. I pull myself up off the floor and see the bath is ready, taps turned off, and waiting. The surface of the water is littered with dead fleas: they abandoned my body for the greater heat of the water.

*

The shambles in the back street. She shuffled through the entry into a wide yard. Rusty plough blades were stacked along one wall, browned grass and dandelions growing around them. On the left the barracks wall, on the right a tall deep shed with a gaping doorway to the murky interior. A cleaver gleamed in the darkness. She felt the metal bite into packed flesh and heard the muffled groan of a beast.

Her legs were ready to give out under her. She forced herself to move forwards, could smell the blood, the guts of the heaving thing. Tasted vomit in the back of her throat. Dizzy now, but falling could see the barracks wall swelling out towards her, felt the air punch her in the ribs, blood flooding eyes, bone shear, gone...

*

The car rolled into the graveyard I got in   I got out   I took shelter under a tree and pulled a book from my pocket.

I browsed the pictures and felt the earth rearrange itself under me: a bumpy bed of restless sleepers. A reader on swamps and bogs: a passage by Jung, recalling dinner with Freud   why are you so concerned with these corpses?   It is a process of natural mummification   humic acid   the bodies are pressed flat by the weight of the peat

Those flattened heads   Heaney's forceps babies   all this talk of death: you have a death wish towards me   it is the black tide of mud that I see swallowing me up

Bremen, 1909   Freud faints

dinner is over

Sigmund you're crazy   There is a *nostalgie de la boue* that we can enjoy   wallow in if you will   Carl, you have a spook complex and it warps all of your theories

In 1971, Joseph Beuys will run into a bog until he disappears: only his signature hat can be seen floating on the dark waters.

And the leathery men they find preserved in the peat? Would-be kings: pretenders with no credentials. They buried them on the borders of the lands they failed to conquer:

Oldcroghan Man was found during the excavation of a drain along what is now a townland and parish boundary, once the territorial boundary between Tuath Cruacháin and Tuath na Cille (a townland is a parish subdivision; Tuath is often translated as 'tribe'). Wondering if this was coincidental, Eamonn Kelly (keeper of antiquities at the National Museum of Ireland) noted that Clonycavan Man, though the precise find spot is unknown, had been found where three baronies meet on the county border between Meath and Westmeath, which separated the ancient territories of Brega and Mide.

Kelly looked at other bog bodies. Two dated iron age bodies had been found close to barony boundaries (baronies are typically county subdivisions), and one actually on one (and a county boundary); a fourth had been found close to a parish boundary. Further research revealed that over forty bog bodies – most of them likely to be iron age – had been found on important boundaries, mainly barony.

The bodies were disfigured – in particular the nipples were sliced off. It's thought custom dictated that subjects of a king would kiss or suck on his nipples as a sign of submission and an acknowledgement of his protection. And so to remove a man's nipples was a signal that they were not worthy to rule.

The peat preserves the evidence and preserves the bodies. The uncanny detail of the corpses collapse time and links us with immediacy to that era. It is a world of warriors, the ancestors of later Christians such as Columba who embrace a new religion and new customs while retaining the old fighting habits. He and his monks embrace the lifestyle of the desert fathers in Egypt (and the Coptic texts in Ireland demonstrate that Eastern link). But they lack deserts and turn to the oceans and the sea paths surrounding Ireland and the Hebrides instead. And, of course, they turn to the bogs: 'We have no prairies to slice a big sun at evening... our pioneers keep striking inwards and downwards', as Heaney put it.

And that same blinding sun defeats us unless we use a disc of blackened glass to view it: its power so strong Christians equate it with the face of God: ‘For now we see through a glass, darkly; but then face to face: now I know in part; but then shall I know even as also I am known.’

The dark pools of the bog function similarly as our pioneers strike inwards, pulling us under the surface and through time. They allow us to see beyond the superficial: we discover alternative worlds beneath. The objects preserved – the relics – work against our daily conception of time. All religious relics work in a similar way – the Cathach of St Columba and the Book of Kells work ostensibly as ‘treasures’ but much more powerfully as portals through time. The Cathach, with its transcription of the *Psalms* reflects Columba’s warrior spirit, as that book dwells on enemies and God’s help under siege. The *Psalms* focus on material, political concerns: ‘He teacheth my hands to war, so that a bow of steel is broken by mine arms.’ The real power, though, lies in the damaged parchment itself, its passage through time and its ability to transport us to Iona in the middle ages.

‘Mirrors should think longer before they reflect’, remarked Jean Cocteau. He had once devised a mirror from a bath filled with mercury and, as his actors disappeared through it, they emerged in the underworld, as if in a dream.

When the poet H.D. visited Freud in 1933 she noticed the ancient Roman and Greek objects that formed a collection in his consulting-room:

Automatically, I walk through the door. It closes. Sigmund Freud does not speak... I look around the room. A lover of Greek art, I am automatically taking stock of the room's contents. Pricelessly lovely objects are displayed here on the shelves to right, to left of me... no one had told me that this room was lined with treasures. I was to greet the Old Man of the Sea, but no one had told me of the treasures he had salvaged from the sea-depth... waiting and finding that I would not or could not speak, he uttered. What he said – and I thought a little sadly – was, 'You are the only person who has ever come into this room and looked at the things in the room before looking at me.'

Later on the couch, she notes:

the exquisite Greek tear-jars and iridescent glass bowls and vases that gleamed in the dusk from the shelves of the cabinet that faced me where I stretched, propped up on the couch in the room in Berggasse 19, Wien IX. The dead were living in so far as they lived in memory or were recalled in dream.

And in the graveyard I heard a voice behind the tree   the centuries flow in different currents beneath the surface   you have made a home now among us   time please.

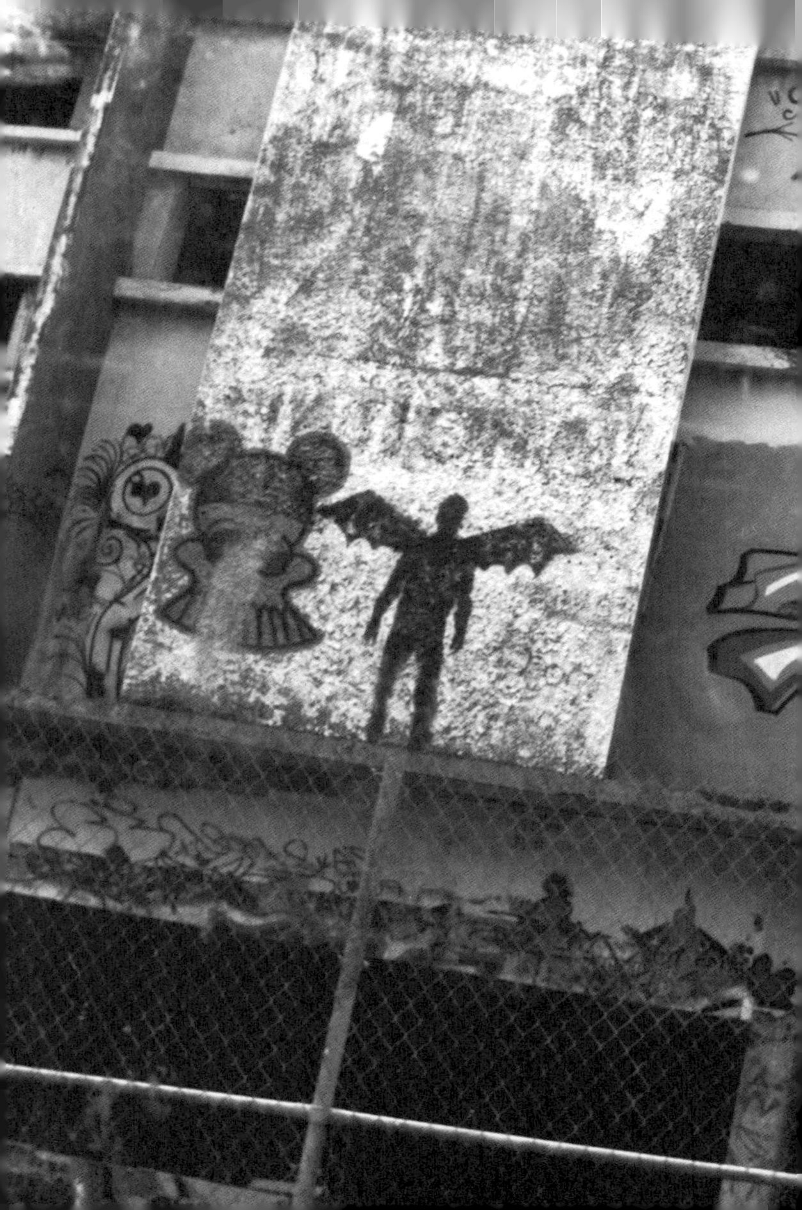

October

She was sitting in a plastic chair in the centre of the room, chain-smoking and staring at the ceiling. As soon as I came in she shifted her gaze and examined me intently.

'What do you need?'

The directness of the question threw me.

'I need...?'

Nothing came out of my mouth. She stood up and walked over to a counter where she pressed the remains of a cigarette into a glass ashtray. Then she lit another, watching me through a cloud of smoke, waving a match quickly in her right hand to extinguish it. Another thin grey plume of smoke streamed from the match before she tossed it into the ashtray.

'You need to talk.'

'No, I'm just thinking how to answer your question – what do I need...'

'No, you need to talk. To her'

She pointed to the girl sitting in the plastic chair.

'Listen to what she says. The first thing you

hear will be her voice. Anything after that is just your own thoughts.'

She drew on the cigarette, held the smoke in her body for a long moment and exhaled: 'Trust the first voice.'

I walked over to the girl in the plastic chair and shivered when I crouched down near her, bringing myself to look into her eyes. She stared back at me with curiosity, observing my fear. I felt a voice in my head: *Anna.*

this is what you can do you can get in a car and you can drive but you will not outrun me if you are afraid and you will not lose me if you need my help I am with you I am inside you much of the time you will think I am you and you will find it difficult to trust my voice or to hear my voice clearly above the commotion of your own thoughts even now we can both hear the police sirens outside as they pass the buildings we are here together this is something you must learn to live with *I am not here for casual conversations and I am not here to help you with some kind of superficial magic or to impress your friends this is a deeper journey and you will change you will lose yourself and what you become will not be who you are now I don't want to say it's too late to stop but having come this far you already know in your heart that things are changing what will happen to you? you will open up and sense the innate movements of the people around you, become more sensitive to their fears, anxieties, joys, secrets you will see beyond their masks and into their hearts you will not just understand them or sympathise with them you will on some level become them even those you don't like or can't approve of this is becoming a wisp of smoke, dispersed on the breeze, part of everything you are here because you want this process, something in you has moved forwards to another point and left behind the old life   you will sense the small lives that surround you – the insects and the cats, dogs and birds and they will recognise you, you will become part of something greater than yourself and your own life will become meaningless I will try to keep you from losing your mind though at times your will mistake me for the illness your fear*

I still hadn't found out the medium's name. She started in the middle of things and just carried on. It seemed rude to ask, and oddly so, given that we were so far beyond the boundaries of normal behaviour.

We sat in the middle of the room – Anna, the medium and myself – in a triangle. The medium was chain-smoking and staring at me. Anna, head down, had her hands folded in her lap. She was very still and I could see her breathing deeply, regularly. Sometimes, though, a tremor ran through her and she seemed to fight to keep her body under control. At these moments she seemed to be shivering in an imperceptible draught – as if each limb were fighting to contain separate spasms, unconnected to each other. It was quietly monstrous.

The medium watched me looking at Anna.

'You need to see beyond the surface you've created here.'

'You mean she doesn't exist – or I know she's... but she is... was... a real person'.

'She was but what you're seeing is probably an image of her from a certain time in her life that suits you both. In a way, you both chose it – you're a man so maybe you need a pretty girl and she will flatter you?'

'Can't you see her?'

'No', she replied, flicking her cigarette against

the edge of an ashtray. 'I'm not a visual medium, it's auditory for me and a sense of their mood that I feel down here.' She rubbed her stomach affectionately and looked again towards Anna's chair. 'I've no idea what you're seeing but I can tell you like her. Typical.'

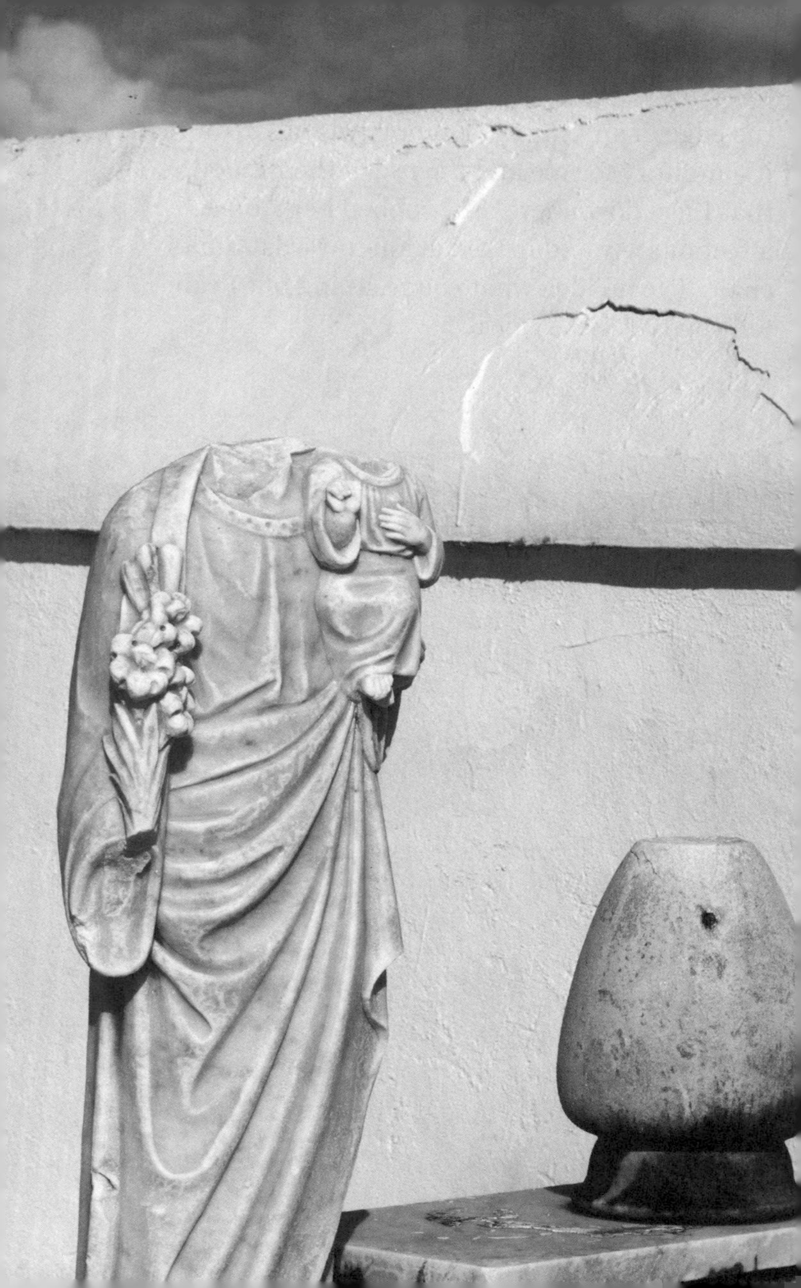

November

I'm waiting to board at the airport and a guard walks past with a SIG rifle and a walkie-talkie on her hip. Voices are crackling and buzzing in static around her body. A man sitting across the room from me is talking earnestly to no one and when he turns his head I see the hands-free earpiece.

On my laptop screen I move a file and discover an open Skype window beneath it on the desktop. A man sits motionless at a desk staring at me. Dead eyes. Silent. Fuzzy pixels blur the image: it's syrupy slow and it warps. Still, it could be a police interrogation cell, or someone in an online chat room waiting for a customer. He seems to be looking straight at me and he says something. I can't lip read, but it looks serious.

*

San Juan, Puerto Rico. The plane descends in a fierce storm. Rain floods the roads, cars plough into fresh rivers of water, junctions float under stop lights. The apartment in Beta Local is dark and hot even though a ceiling fan is working overtime. Sleeping like a lamb through the apocalypse I wake up in Calle Luna and find great coffee in a café just around the corner.

Gradually I get settled and meet everyone. After a week I give a lecture, ranging from spirit photography and Achsa Sprague to the Beatles and the British roots of psychedelia. This seems popular and over the coming days people turn up and lend me books on spiritism in Puerto Rico. White table espiritismo is the term they use and point me towards the influence of a French writer, Allan Kardec, whose books seem vital to the spread of spiritism in the Caribbean in the late-nineteenth century. The 'White Table' has its origins in the use of white tablecloths and, implicitly, the middle-class membership of these spiritist churches.

At first I'm confused as this all sounds like spiritualism and reading around it I find that Kardec was initially attracted to that movement. His own work though – developed as 'spiritism' – has some significant differences. There is an emphasis on reincarnation and his approach to the subject has a scientific flavour – spiritism is a science dedicated to the relationship between spirits and human beings.

Spiritism spread quickly across the globe, taking root particularly in Latin America – Argentina, Uruguay, Cuba, Brazil and Puerto Rico. Just as spiritualism had allied itself to emerging causes such as women's suffrage and the abolition of slavery, spiritism became embedded in political movements that challenged traditional power structures and labour relations.

One of the most spectacular examples of this combined religious and political force manifested itself in Catalonia where spiritist-anarchist groups bloomed across the region from the 1860s until the 1930s. At the end of the Spanish Civil War, the fascist state closed all spiritist centres, imprisoning or executing many of the activists linked to them.

The Spanish poet and anthropologist, Gerard Horta, has traced the history of this particular regional manifestation of spiritism in his book *De la mística a les barricades*. There he points to the influence of the Catalan strain of mystical utopianism as it was outlined in the 'First International Spiritist Congress' in Barcelona in 1888.

An audience of global delegates were treated to a wide discussion of topics that included:

* the acknowledgment of spiritism as a positive science – psychological and social – and at the same time as a 'secular religion'
* the vindication of gender equality and the emancipation of women
* the promotion of secular education in order to transform society on the basis of charity, reason, justice and law
* the need for a prison reform aiming at the social reintegration of prisoners
* the complete rejection of war industry
* the call for a social, political and cultural revolution that would originate in the inner self of the individual
* the pressing need for cooperativism as a way of organizing production and reconciling the forces of capital and labour...

There were also calls for:

* the worldwide abolition of slavery
* the gradual elimination of political borders
* the gradual disarmament of permanent armies by means of spoken word and the press

* the secularisation of cemeteries
* the introduction of a unified and compulsory birth certificate
* the introduction of civil marriage
* the abolition of the death penalty and life imprisonment
* the role of cosmopolitism as a guiding principle for social relations
* the promotion of universal communion and solidarity between all beings

Delegates from Puerto Rico attended the Congress and it's clear that a similar engagement between spiritism, or 'espiritismo', and anarchism took hold on the island. Even so, the prominent anarchist organiser Luisa Capetillo still felt she had to defend that fusion. In an article entitled *¿Anarquista y Espiritista?... ¡Uf, Uf!* she stresses the quasi scientific character of spiritism and its implicit challenge to the established social order:

> *I don't see why the scientific concept of spiritism should be opposed to that of Anarchy. The direction of both is a matter of more or less passionate temperaments. If we were to take spiritism along the path of violence,*

it would lose its superiority as a philosophical concept. Anarchy doesn't promote violence either. Anarchy states that no one has the right to govern or exploit another, or to monopolise the land or tools of labour. It also states that no individual should hold a job that goes against his or her aspirations, preferences or convenience. Nor should any two people who are repulsive to each other be forced to cohabitate. They should be free to be together or apart. Which of the anarchist objectives does Spiritism reject?

This organic attraction of anarchists and spirits brings me back to the first statements made by the medium in Glasgow when I attended the spiritualist church: her challenge to the established social system in every respect and just as importantly a challenge aimed at the organisation of everyday reality, not just a revolt against a particular policy or regime...

And so now, in a non-descript suburb of San Juan, I'm sitting in a backyard that seems to recede into jungle. Dogs are barking everywhere and I understand suddenly that the yard would be impossible to breach with this organic alarm system. Someone is explaining that anarchists in Puerto Rico have always frequented the white table houses. This anarchist's parents both were spiritualists and spoke to the dead on a daily basis. Spiritism was the first in a series of conversions that led to faith in Che and Fidel, then the extremes of the 1970s before a more grounded application of trade unionism and finally a home in the Zapatista movement.

The barking of the dogs reminds me of a visit to Ceiba the day before. There, a vast abandoned US naval station was returning to nature. Trees and plants were closing in on an old cinema. The station was as expansive as a small city. Down the road from the cinema, past empty accommodation blocks and abandoned supermarkets we came to a sport centre. The ceiling of the gymnasium was collapsing, its wooden floor was slowly rotting and giant toads were basking in the derelict swimming pools beyond. All across the fading city, packs of wild dogs patrolled their territories, scattering from time to time in the wake of startled wild horses. The base had been used to support aircraft carriers that moored in the harbour and launched planes towards the island of Vieques, converting much of it into an irradiated bombing range for sixty years. We walked the piers that serviced the carriers. They appeared to stretch to infinity, taking us far out into the sea at a dizzying height above the waves. At the end there was nothing but the sun falling into the ocean like one more nuclear device.

Back in San Juan, it made sense to take refuge in a bar. Weariness kicks in. Behind the counter, in a corner, there's a statue of a cross-legged Indian Chief, a cigar in his lap, flanked by two tall glasses of Sauza Hacienda tequila and a large jar stuffed with dollars. What is that anyway? *An altar...* A little TV screen is suspended above, silently transmitting old catwalk shows. This one starts with two robotic arms emerging from the darkness, sliding up and down the walkway on rails – McQueen. *Plato's Atlantis...* That's perfect. It's raining outside. Lights out, boys, lights out.

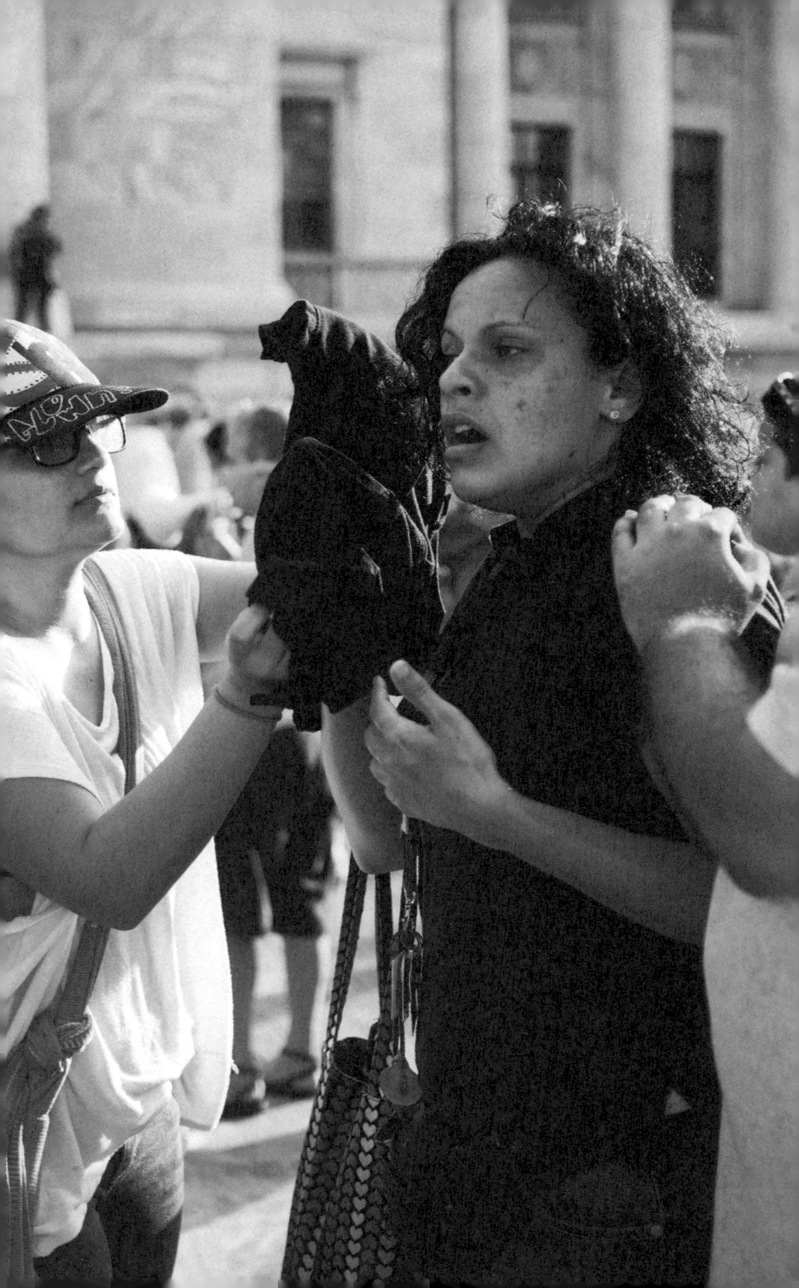

December

Behind the wall of the city he can still hear the chant of the protesters – '¡La lucha sigue! ¡La lucha sigue!' He walks into the sea, face to the shore, the waves beating against his back. Slowly, finding his way backwards to keep his footing on the rocks and sand beneath, he feels the switch – the pull of the sea outwards rather than the surge towards land. Then the floor disappears until he lets himself sink and continues walking. He flails against the darkness and feels the weight overwhelm him. Pain and blackness explode. And then the flood of voices surrounds him and in the cold darkness he feels the mass of bodies lifting him with them as they surge forwards and out onto the land and the burst of noise breaching the waves '¡La lucha sigue!'

The word I hear most in San Juan is 'syncretic', referring to the fusion of two religious systems. Slaves from various regions of the African continent and taken to the Caribbean decided to combine the gods from their religions. It was illegal to worship those gods and the Catholic Church strictly imposed their own pantheon of saints. Soon, each African Orisha was linked to a Christian saint so that both could be worshipped – one visibly, one secretly. Changó, for instance, the god of Bata drums, master of dance, god of lightning, thunder and fire was linked to Saint Barbara, while Elegguá the trickster, god of the crossroads, was linked to Saint Anthony.

Underpinning the survival of the African gods were the drums. Each god has a distinct rhythmic pattern, played out on Bata drums, sacred within the religion. The same drum patterns also underpin the music that laid the foundations of Cuban and Puerto Rican salsa, morphing into something less folkloric and coolly commercial. The percussionist Mongo Santamaría is a good example of how those rhythms were introduced to a broader audience. He issued a series of folkloric albums towards the end of the 1950s – *Changó* (1954), *Yambú* (1958), *Mongo* (1959), and *Bembé* (1960) while also experimenting with afro-jazz on tunes like 'Afro-Blue' and 'Watermelon Man'.

Tony in Beta Local explains to me how drumming was central to the legendary band leader Rafael Cortijo, who moved his drums to the front of the stage, emphasising their rhythms alongside the radical shock of a black band breaking into television and white consciousness. Cortijo's lead singer, Ismael Rivera, went on to achieve the kind of immortality normally associated with Bob Marley. In San Juan, murals of 'Maelo' still appear in the streets, his solo albums are totemic and his life follows a trajectory of rise to fame, fall to prison, drugs, and a struggle for redemption. On one of his best albums, *Lo Ultima de la Avenida*, Rivera presents an explicit demonstration of the relation between the sacred rhythms of Santeria and salsa in a song called 'Cantar Maravilloso'. It begins in a strictly folkloric vein with drums and voice only, a timeless moment. Then, after a brief pause, a horn section and classic salsa piano take over. That transition is a reminder of where the music springs from and the pause between the two sections of the song opens a door into a history that encompasses religion, slavery, trade, empire and a secret life in the hills.

The owner of a botánica opens a parcel on the counter, flattens the white tissue paper gingerly and peers with curiosity that equals my own at the black object revealed. It's a coconut head: a black shock of hair, raw as a new brush, and two big white teeth askew in the mouth. One of the eyes has broken open and seeds are streaming out. She laughs, pushes the head towards me and shouts 'Boo!'

A chalk-white egg in a tray of water with a red glass candle: it looks good, even beautiful. I'm learning how to make small altars using some sliced apples, chicken meat and white rum. Different Orishas have different tastes: Ogún might prefer a baked sweet potato and some molasses, Changó is partial to fried okra, rum seems a constant... Special candles you can buy in the supermarket.

And then the flood of voices surrounds him and in the cold darkness he feels the mass of bodies lifting him with them as they surge forwards and out onto the land and the burst of noise breaching the waves '¡La lucha sigue!' He flails against the darkness and feels the weight overwhelm him. Pain and blackness explode. Then the floor disappears until he lets himself sink and continues walking. Slowly, finding his way backwards to keep his footing on the rocks and sand beneath, he feels the switch – the pull of the sea outwards rather than the surge towards land. He walks into the sea, face to the shore, the waves beating against his back.

Behind the wall of the city he can still hear the chant of the protesters – '¡La lucha sigue! ¡La lucha sigue!'

Michy takes me to L'Alquimista, a bar on Calle San Agustín in Puerta de Tierra. Actually it looks more like a shop. There is a counter but it's filled with antiques, paintings, lamp shades and vinyl albums... The pool table is also stacked high with albums and the owner, Wiso Ayala, watches me sort through the vinyl hoard. As I pick out old classic salsa albums – Ray Barretto, Oscar D'Leon, Héctor Lavoe, Cheo Feliciano, some so obvious – Celia Cruz and Willie Colón, Ismael Rivera, even one by Eddie Palmieri – he gets the drift. There's a large cardboard box sitting at the back of the bar: it's full of photographs. We sit down, and Wiso begins to talk me through the pictures – DJs, early photos of Cortijo, local promoters and bar owners. He picks a CD – *Ricanstruction* by Ray Barretto and blasts it out on a little hi-fi system. Two old men come to the entrance, drawn by the music, and watch us sort through the pictures and the albums.

Eventually I have nearly forty LPs. Wiso promises he has far more at home and that he'll bring them on Thursday. It's hot, I'm Irish and I'm weighed down with masses of vinyl as I head back to Beta Local. Then I hear protest chants coming from the Senate Building so I slowly, sweatily divert in that direction. It's a mass demonstration by the teachers' union. I'd seen them already through the last week, picketing outside the Senate about their pensions that were about to be cut. Now they were out en masse and pressing against a police line on the steps of the Senate.

Two women who have set up a speculative drinks stand for the protestors agree to look after my albums, bemused by the stack of ancient hits. Just as I approach the police line with my camera a rainstorm burst from nowhere. Everyone looks up and scatters in confusion. Suddenly there seems to be a breach in the police line and protestors are surging towards the doors of the Senate. I follow, trying to catch the scenes as the doors give way. There's a burst of mist and people are screaming and the tide turns taking me back down the steps with it. A woman howling, tears and rain pouring down her face, friends with towels swabbing her eyes. Pepper spray. I'm still wondering how the line broke and let the protestors get just so far when a man in a suit pushes through the crowd and waves a police badge at me – 'We support this protest. What is happening the teachers will happen to us next!' I take the photograph.

I've heard several times that there is a near-mythical hoard of salsa vinyl in a ferretería, or ironmongery shop. It's in Calle Roberts in Santurce and you have to ring to enter. Inside it's obvious why you need to request entry as the shop is stocked like an encyclopaedia of nuts, bolts, tools, pots and pans: theft would be simple if the door wasn't locked. The old owner takes me down through aisles of saws, drills, screws and torches and proudly points me to a parallel world of vinyl. He tells me about his child-hood, moving from one airbase to another across the US with his father. He explains the rough system of classification for the hundreds of record stacks and leaves me there for several hours. *Homenaje a Yemaya* by Celia Cruz is in the first stack I dig into…

I'm standing on the beach surrounded by thousands of people drawn to the shouts of the crowd beyond the city wall: '¡La lucha sigue! ¡La lucha sigue!' We all walk backwards towards the sea and the tide draws us down into the deep. I am pulled under with the others as the sea floor drops away suddenly and there is an almighty howl as we plunge into the abyss. Blackness momentarily overwhelms me as the oxygen rips from my flailing body and then I'm rising, soaring up towards the moonlight. I breach the surface sucking in air and find my footing as I surge forwards towards land. I can hear a multitude of voices in my head and from above, beyond the wall, '¡La lucha sigue! ¡La lucha sigue!'

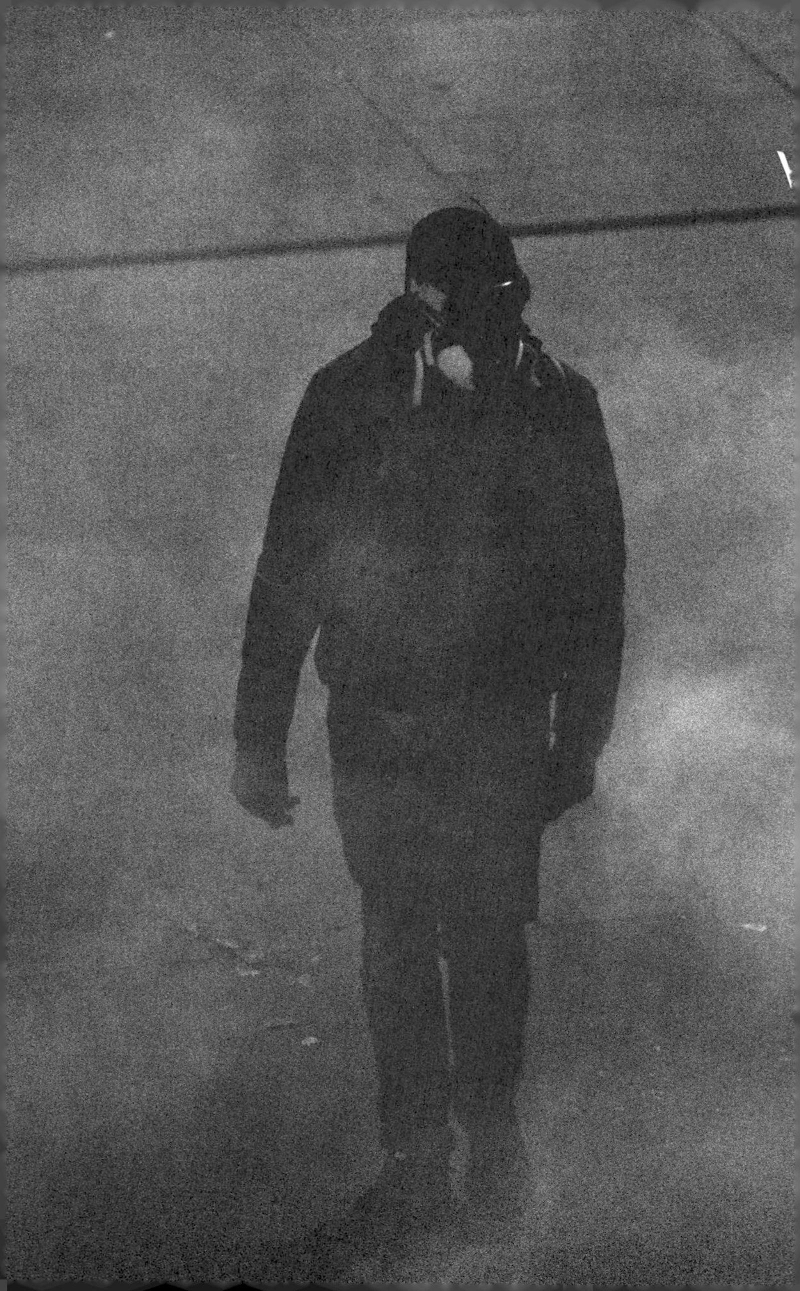

Postscript

There's a door that you can walk through and reemerge into the avenue just beyond the riot squad, somewhere between the Crowne Plaza and Monop. There, you find a strange mixture of onlookers: the elderly comparing today's tactics with their own back in 1968; tourists adapting selfie sticks to periscope above the police line; and even stranded protestors caught by surprise outside the field of combat.

It takes time to adjust. Tear gas still burns the air, and dense red smoke rises above the fray, shrouding a black cross flag. A policeman thinks I'm spending too much time studying the whole situation and asks me to open my backpack. I'm as curious as he is so we both investigate... It seems I'm a changed man: one small baguette, six oranges and some shelled pistachios. There's also a camera and a new deck of cards in the front pouch – the tarot de Marseille by Jean Dodal. Leaving nothing to chance I shuffle to find the one I'm looking for: The Hanged Man.

In the Marseille deck he hangs upside down by his left leg while the right leg is bent at the knee making an L shape or an inverted 4. Although he's dressed in a blue body stocking, his right leg is green, a similar colour to the two trees that flank him tightly. The trees have been thoroughly pruned and the branch stumps are bright red. With his wild blond hair almost brushing the ground, the hanged man's head is a dropped sun and like a good sex pistol, his tongue sticks out defiantly.

He seems suspended from the sky itself. Today I think he's Odin who hung from the tree Yggdrasil for nine days: when he finally saw the runes of wisdom he died, but the power he had received brought him back to life immediately. More bluntly, upside down, cradled within those blood-red stumps he looks like a child about to be born.

'One card, one question' they say. But that's not really true. Every card evokes another. The Hanged Man reminds me of The Judgement where the dead rise like sprouting plants charmed by a blond herald angel: as he readies his trumpet he sticks his tongue out just like the gallows tree punk. I get the message.

Across the square I can see the usual mixed crowd of people milling around the DIY shrine to the dead of Bataclan. Some tourists, teenagers, the occasional street hustler. There are also some wary black bloc wannabe anarchists who are keeping a sceptical distance from the Nuit Debout meetings sprawled across the rest of the Place de la République. They're waiting for nightfall when the police will join them in a ritual, tear-gassed choreography.

Closer to the main forum of the protest there are two lines of stands, booths and makeshift tents, each occupied by a different issue: anti-specism, veganism, the Greek economy, Peruvian prisoners, rent control, alternative education, LGBTI rights, Guyanese politics, French sign language and many more. There are variations of Debout – Pierreux Debout, Biblio Debout, Ecology Debout. Each group has at least one table and each table is covered with handouts anchored against the wind by stones.

Flitting among these groups I'm drawn to one off to the side, under the trees. Cross-legged on the ground there is a serious young woman taking copious notes, while an odd mix of

Asian, African and French protesters sitting around her appear to argue over the growth of cities.

'The future is Shanghai or Guangzhou –'

'– or Paris...'

'Not Paris!'

'Why not? It might be a different future than China's, no sci-fi steel and glass towers but...'

'There are many futures moving at different speeds in different places'

'– is about growth, but we need to understand the psychology of growth –'

Anna is sitting beside the earnest young woman, watching her work, smiling at me when she catches my eye.

(it's about time)

'...the wave-length of the human time-span...'

(well, I just arrived...)

(no. I'm saying it's all about time)

(time past and time present, east coker, all of that?)

'– what we have now is urban spectacle entangled with prophecy…'

(yes all of that.)

'…there is no oxygen on the moon, and democracy in Europe is scarce too'

(it's about your trace in time… others lock into that and form a continuum)

'you need to know the flics are using a trombinoscope to help them pick people up'

I sense an almost indiscernible shift in mood sweeping across the square. Irregular bands of marchers have been merging from the metro for a while and, most oddly, many of them are sneezing. Suddenly everyone is wary and, as if telepathically, they look in unison toward the treetops.

They see the contrails of tear gas arc across the square. They can hear the canisters clatter on paving stones and the hiss as they spin like fireworks into the crowds of protestors. For a split second no one reacts: the gas billows upwards through a still tableaux of people on pause. Then, the freeze-frame jerks back into motion and we break away fast: the white bitter clouds drift west while everyone runs south. Riot police retreat at the edge of the square but regroup and chase us through a labyrinth of small streets.

The intimacy is always surprising. Out of the blue, people begin to give directions and work together to guide each other through the smoke. Stranger still is the intimate relationship with the riot police. You quickly get to recognise them. Some are brutal, some are human: their eyes still give them away, even shielded by visors.

Time stretches too. I'm beginning to see Anna's point. I may be racing down an alley but when I catch the sound of early Wailers from a window ('the stone that the builder refuse will always be the head cornerstone...') some kind of sonic trapdoor opens to Jamaica in 1970. It's only an instant and I'm still running, rounding a corner, heading further into the Marais district now but that sound is still spreading through my brain, working in its own timeframe while I'm processing shouts, rapid changes of direction and the tell-tale hiss of gas canisters on the pavement.

Time truly slows in rue Rambuteau when we run into walls of riot shields. We're lined against the windows of a bookshop, it's shut but I can see Anna inside, browsing the shelves while I stand for nearly an hour waiting to be processed. An attic window opens high above me and coloured water bombs fall into the street. A banner drops into the wind, writhing at the end of strings. Scrawled across it, 'Without debate, democracy is a dead star.' Beyond the checkpoint, shoppers with customised carrier bags rubberneck as they flow past in this unreal city. Time for Glasgow.

List of images

All images by Francis McKee.

Common Objectives is a series of projects from artist/writer collectives or individual art practices engaged with emerging political struggles, rejecting the idea of culture as a playground for the elite, engaging in the potent mix of free discourse, solidarity and the production of new desires and prepared to break open old worlds, either in the virtual space of communication and networks, or in the concrete world of action, discourse and distribution.

Even the Dead Rise Up by Francis McKee

This publication is published as part of *Common Objectives*, commissioned by Book Works from open submission and edited by Nina Power and Gavin Everall.

Published and distributed by Book Works

Commissioning Editor Nina Power

Proofreading by Gerrie van Noord

Designed by Erik Hartin and Moa Pårup

Cover image: *Le Jugement*, Jean Dodal, Lyon, *c.* 1701. Reprinted by Jean-Claude Flornoy.

Typeset in Miller Text and House Holiday Gothic. Cover typeface: Berthold Akzidenz Grotesk using letters from Akzidenz Grotesk Harlequin by Europa, courtesy Europa.

Printed by Aldgate Press in London using Arcoprint Edizioni Avorio 1.7; 70gsm and Freelife Vellum White 260g.

Book Works receives National Portfolio funding from Arts Council England. This publication is generously supported by Creative Scotland.

ISBN 978 1 906012 59 5

Book Works
19 Holywell Row
London EC2A 4JB
www.bookworks.org.uk
telephone: +44 (0)207 247 2203

Supported using public funding by ARTS COUNCIL ENGLAND

ALBA | CHRUTHACHAIL